HELP IN TIME OF NEED

Help in Time of Need

Encouragement, Practical Advice, and Prayers

Ronda Chervin, Ph.D.

CHARIS

Servant Publications
Ann Arbor, Michigan

Charis Books is an imprint of Servant Publications especially designed to serve Roman Catholics.

Servant Publications Mission Statement
We are dedicated to publishing books that spread the gospel of Jesus Christ, help Christians to live in accordance with that gospel, promote renewal in the church, and bear witness to Christian unity.

Servant Publications
P.O. Box 8617
Ann Arbor, MI 48107
www.servantpub.com

Cover design: Paul Higdon, Minneapolis, Minn.

02 03 04 05 10 9 8 7 6 5 4 3 2 1

Printed in the United States of America
ISBN 1-56955-285-1

Library of Congress Cataloging-in-Publication Data

Chervin, Ronda.
   Help in time of need : encouragement, practical advice, and prayers /
Ronda Chervin.
     p. cm.
   Includes bibliographical references and index.
   ISBN 1-56955-285-1 (alk. paper)
   1. Consolation. 2. Christian life--Catholic authors. 3.
Suffering--Religious aspects--Catholic Church. I. Title.
   BX2373.S5 C48 2002
   248.8'6--dc21

                                         2002005999

～ *Contents* ～

~ Introduction ~

Cast all your anxieties on him, for he cares about you.

1 PETER 5:7

"I feel overwhelmed!" "I can't cope!" These are words I say and hear more and more often. Life is truly overwhelming, especially if you add to your own burdens those of the rest of the world with all its injustices, starting with the victimized unborn. To feel in control in the face of such tragedies would be whistling in the dark.

The opposite of being overwhelmed could be the sense that everything is going great. But for the faithful, even when everything is not going great, the answer is always to turn to the One who proclaimed that he is "the way, and the truth, and the life" (Jn 14:6).

Well, you might be thinking, there's overwhelming, and then there's *overwhelming!* I wonder whether Ronda Chervin really knows what I am going through.

I could give you credentials such as a Ph.D. in Catholic philosophy; an M.A. in Religious Studies; experience as a professor in several universities; more than fifty published books; and lectures all over the world. Those would be adequate credentials for writing many books. But for *Help in Time of Need,* the major source of credibility would be what sufferings I have survived with the help of the Lord.

Within the course of about six years, beginning in 1987, I experienced these losses: the natural deaths of my mother, father, husband,

and godparents; the loss of my son by suicide; the loss of a breast to cancer; the loss of my home to an earthquake; and the loss of a job to marginalization. Pretty heavy!

The ways that God, Mary, the angels and saints, family, and friends helped me survive and even flourish are what I want to share with you in the chapters to follow. Truly, as we used to say in the early days of the charismatic renewal: "Jesus and I are bigger than my problems!"

Each of the first eight chapters will address a specific problem you may be dealing with. There will be a short, totally fictional description of someone who feels overwhelmed. This description will be followed by a reflection.

The reflection will be an expression of my perspective on Catholic truth. Sometimes it will seem to you to be right on. At other times you might question what I write. That is fine. It should lead you to do your own praying to see whether Jesus is teaching you a complementary truth. For each problem there will also be a prayer, along with Scripture texts for meditation.

The last three chapters will lead you towards comfort and wisdom through quiet times of Eucharistic adoration; prayers asking for the intercession of Mary, the angels, and saints; and opening yourself to joy in the new life God wants for you when a crisis is past. Look over the contents carefully. Topics you might think would be in one chapter may be in another. For example, the sudden death of a beloved person is not addressed in the chapter "Help Me, Lord, I Never Saw It Coming!" but in "Wipe Away Our Tears!"

As you begin to read my book, you might like to ponder this message I heard as from the Lord the day I began to write:

The crosses you will write about I permit partly in the hope that sufferers will come closer to me. But instead of casting their cares on me, many spend hours, days, months, and even years mulling things over in their own minds, all the while ignoring my open arms. Life without me is overwhelming. Tell them I am waiting for them to bring their pain to my Sacred Heart.

One

Help Me, Lord, I Never Saw It Coming!

But of that day or that hour no one knows.

MARK 13:32

The context of these words of Jesus, more popularly translated "You know not the day or the hour," is about the coming of the kingdom of God. Yet the phrase is so striking that Christians often recall these words in connection with any sudden misfortune.

Sometimes we think that if we do our part, not committing any big sins, our lives will run along smoothly. Many Scripture passages do tell us about the joys that come with godly living, but none that I know of guarantee a smooth life on earth. I think we would be better off if we imitated those believers of the past who added "God willing" to every sentence about plans for the future.

Each of the following sections contains a narrative, a reflection, a prayer, and a scriptural text. Before you read each section, I suggest you unite yourself in prayer with Jesus and ask him to open you to hear what the Holy Spirit might be saying to you, whether about something past, present, or possibly coming in the future.

I Lost My Job!

Fear not, for I am with you and will bless you.

"As long-time manager of the West Coast office of a nationwide company, I felt pretty secure: $75,000 a year plus commissions. During a recession, we had layoffs. I had to make tough decisions about who should go. Those with poor sales would obviously be dropped. But what about choices between the oldest—close to retirement with the highest pay—and the ones last hired, on low salaries?

"When I tossed and turned in the night about it, my wife consoled me: 'Honey, there's no way to avoid pain for someone. You just have to give it to God. Ask him who will hurt the least.'

"When announcing a layoff I made sure to commend the salesperson for past work and to provide severance and fine recommendations. I tried to do the right thing.

"You can imagine my shock, then, when the CEO of our company came to the West Coast. After the usual fancy lunch, he announced, 'I have some bad news. Due to the last stock dip, we're consolidating. You've been one of our most valuable managers, and we'll give you six months more on salary before laying you off, with a great recommendation.'

"I took a fast walk from the table to the men's room to avoid a response I would have regretted. All the way home I wished I'd said something like this: 'After all the profits I've brought to the company, why don't you fire one of those young know-nothings instead of me?'

"After dinner, I got my wife alone and told her the bad news. Instead of berating me for not finding a clever way to keep my job, she grabbed my hands and asked, 'What did Jesus tell you about this?'"

Reflection and Prayer

The unexpected loss of a job usually feels like a betrayal. Fear of not finding a good new job sometimes makes it hard to pray with confident trust. Eventually, you need to bring the whole experience to the Lord. If you've worked hard and want the best things in life for yourself or family, it's natural to feel devastated at the sudden loss of a job. There is no need to pretend with God that you are so holy such a blow can't hurt you or make you angry.

In trying to arrive at a Christian viewpoint, a father might consider the plight of persecuted Catholics. How would it be to face total destitution and slavery for the family, as has been happening in the Sudan? Wouldn't Jesus want you to offer up some of your pain for fathers in that situation?

The loss of a job by the main wage earner may mean others in the family need to pitch in to bridge the gap between the lost job and the next one. When resentful thoughts start to churn up towards those responsible for the loss of a job, you might try to pray in this way:

"Dear Jesus, you worked as a carpenter with St. Joseph. There were times of insecurity for your foster father, such as the time your family had to leave Bethlehem for Egypt when you were newly born. I offer up to you the anger and fear I'm feeling now. Help me to forgive those responsible.

"Thank you for the good years of the past. Help me believe in your loving plans for me and for those I support. Give me light about contacts for a future job. In solidarity with the truly poor, let me be grateful for any job you send, even if it means a less affluent lifestyle. Help me to use the gifts you have given me to serve future customers and bring profit to a new company."

∼ *Scripture for Meditation* ∼

Naked I came from my mother's womb, and naked shall I return; the Lord gave, and the Lord has taken away; blessed be the name of the Lord.

JOB 1:21

Give us this day our daily bread.

MATTHEW 6:11

And why are you anxious about clothing? Consider the lilies of the field, how they grow; they neither toil nor spin; yet I tell you, even Solomon in all his glory was not arrayed like one of these. But if God so clothes the grass of the field, which today is alive and tomorrow is thrown into the oven, will he not much more clothe you, O men of little faith?

MATTHEW 6:28-30

The Police Are Calling About My Child!

Hear, my son, your father's instruction, and reject not your mother's teaching.

PROVERBS 1:8

"I will never forget those words: 'Are you the mother of Robert Finnegan?'

"'Yes. Who is this? Nothing's happened to my son?'

"'Joe Smith from Orange County Juvenile Hall. Your son's been placed in custody on a drug charge. If you'd like to see him, we'll arrange for a special visitation tonight. His hearing will be in two or three days at the Juvenile Court.'

"My husband and I rushed down to Juvenile Hall. It was the worst moment we ever had as parents. Robert is our oldest. He's fifteen, a sophomore in high school. He's an honor student, a good boy, never giving us any trouble.

"All the way down to Orange my husband drove over the speed limit. He kept grilling me. 'Who was he with? Was it that older boy with the earrings? With my two jobs, I can't know where each of those kids are all the time!'

"'Maybe it's a mistake,' I kept saying, clutching my rosary. 'Robert would never do such a thing.' The high school has a good program with videos about the dangers of drugs and the hard penalties. Every time Robert went out the door in the evening I warned him to stay away from anything bad. Then I prayed that his guardian angel would protect him.

"When we got down to Juvenile Hall, we saw our son was sitting on a bench with his head in his hands. I rushed over and put my arms around him. My husband stood in front of him. He jerked Bobby's head up so he could look into his eyes. 'They said you were picked up on a drug charge. Say it was a mistake!'

"Our son didn't respond. He just lowered his head again. My heart went out to him. 'Bobby, we're here to help you. We'll do everything we can to get you off.'

"An officer came in to explain Robert's situation. Even though he was a minor and it was his first offense, he could be sentenced to ninety days in Juvenile Hall since he was caught selling crack and tested for having it in his own system, too.

"On the way back home I cried and cried."

Reflection and Prayer

Many parents hear on the news or from their neighbors about teens having run-ins with the police, but they think it can't happen to their own children. You may imagine that you know exactly what your children are doing, but there is no way you can watch them every minute unless you make them into prisoners. Even in families of devout Catholics, a teen can get into bad trouble with drugs without the parents' knowledge.

If this has happened in your family, you don't have to feel guilty, as if it must have been your fault. In the case of a miserable surprise like the one in this story, you need to offer up your agony to Jesus, who is no stranger to disappointment.

Remember that the Church can help your troubled child in important ways. It would be good to get in touch immediately with the

Catholic chaplain at the juvenile facility to ask him to offer sacramental confession and counsel. Your child needs to go to Mass in the prison. This may be the time the words of forgiveness in the liturgy would ring the truest for your teen.

Call the office of your diocese and find out how to get in touch with the detention ministry. They visit the prisons regularly to offer in-depth prayer and counsel. Consider that God may have allowed this incident, terrible as it is, as a warning before your child gets into even worse trouble.

You might want to pray with your spouse and the whole family every night before bed in this way:

"Father in heaven, we give you our child in detention. Only you know the pressures he was under when he gave in to temptation. We know that you forgive him. Help us to forgive him for disobeying us.

"Help us not to forget everything good about our child. We ask you to take away shame and give us hope. Help those ministering to him to open him to your love and your ways of wisdom. Keep him away from anyone in prison who can harm him.

"Only you can tear out the roots of his weaknesses. Still, if we need to change our ways of parenting, give us insight and grace to do so."

~ *Scripture for Meditation* ~

[Give] knowledge and discretion to the youth.

PROVERBS 1:4

All day long my disgrace is before me, and shame has covered my face.

PSALM 44:15

Hope in God; for I shall again praise him, my help and my God.

PSALM 43:5

How Could Anyone in My Family Make Such a Bad Choice?

Do you not see that whatever goes into a man from outside cannot defile him...? For from within, out of the heart of man, come evil[s].... They defile a man.

MARK 7:18, 21, 23

"Now, this! I never saw it coming that my oldest daughter, Trish, so smart and pretty, would pick out such a guy to fall in love with and get engaged to.

"He came to our home the first time on his motorcycle. With the tattoos, ponytail, and heavy metal, we assumed he was lost. When I saw Trish running downstairs, I grabbed her and pulled her into the kitchen.

"'Who is this character?'

"'He calls himself Tiger.'

"'Where did you meet him?'

"'At a dance at the community college.'

"'What do you know about him?'

"'He's a Christian, Dad. He has a cross tattooed on his heart!'

"Surprised and slightly reassured, I walked outside to make sure the guy had a helmet for Trish. I took down Tiger's phone number and politely told him to bring her back by midnight.

"Six months later you can imagine our amazement when she invited us out to dinner and Tiger showed up. Sitting next to him, beaming and holding his hand, Trish made the big announcement.

"'Tiger and I are engaged. We'll be married a year from now when I graduate and Tiger saves up enough for a first and last on an apartment. I know he doesn't look like my type, but he has a heart of gold, and I know you're going to love him, too.'"

Reflection and Prayer

Parents tend to assume their children will associate with, and eventually marry, people a lot like themselves: of the same religion, the same economic bracket, and with similar lifestyles. So fixed are the habits of groups in society that small differences may become red flags. A woman drinking beer out of a can rather than a glass can signify crudity to one group, but flair to another. A man with a ponytail signifies drug abuse to some people, but individuality to others.

The suspicions may run both directions. It can take many years for in-law families to understand and appreciate each other's ways. No doubt the families of the fiancés of your children will find certain things about your family objectionable, or maybe just stiff and overly conventional.

If Jesus came to your door with long hair and a full beard, would you turn him away? What about the disciples with bare feet? Or a Franciscan with dirty clothes?

As you read these questions, you are probably thinking that in former times these manners were more common. In our times many men with ponytails are on drugs, and dirty clothes more likely come from slovenliness than from evangelical poverty. Just the same, it is important before coming to conclusions about the men and women your children marry to distinguish between these two sets of traits: habits of little significance we should ignore or might even come to find amusing, and vices we should come against, usually not with unwanted advice, but certainly in the prayer of spiritual warfare.

This prayer might help you bring your genuine concerns to the Lord:

"Dear Jesus, you love the person my child has chosen to marry just as much as you love each of us. Help me to see this new person the way you do. Let me trust that even if the negative traits of my child's spouse will cause suffering, you have allowed this to happen as part of your loving plan for them.

"May my own child be purified of traits that will bring pain to his or her spouse. If there are any ways of thinking, feeling, and acting coming down our family trees that will impact badly on this marriage, I ask now for healing and deliverance. I know you want our family to be a miniature kingdom of God, full of love.

"Forgive me for any harsh or mistaken judgments about the character of the one who loves my child. Each time one of the trivial habits of this person upsets me, help me not to overreact."

∼ *Scripture for Meditation* ∼

Judge not, that you be not judged.

MATTHEW 7:1

Do not judge by appearances.

JOHN 7:24

You judge according to the flesh, I judge no one.

JOHN 8:15

Pregnant in *My* Circumstances?

The Lord called me from the womb, from the body of my mother he named my name.

ISAIAH 49:1

"'I come today, Jesus, with a heavy heart,' 'I wrote recently in my journal. I feel bewildered. Why did you let it happen? We were so faithful to the sacrifices of natural family planning, not like all those contracepting couples around us. Just one time we took a slight chance on our twentieth wedding anniversary.

"'You know how old and tired I feel after the five births and those miscarriages in between. Before this baby is born I'll be forty-two, with rebellious teens still in the house driving me crazy.'

"When I got quiet enough to listen to a word from the Lord in my heart, I got not words, but an image of him as he opened his arms with a big smile on his beautiful face. Still upset, I went to see Ramona, a friend in my women's prayer group. She has seven children.

"She told me she and her husband were also surprised when the last child was conceived. Her husband was depressed and suggested giving the baby up for adoption. Hugging her two-year-old tot, Ramona told me this little one is now the joy of the family.

"Because she is too tired to take care of everything, the teen boys help more than usual. The oldest daughter, who seemed to hate living in a big family before, started to blossom as she helped mother her baby sister. Because she and her husband are older, they find parenting different from before. No longer so worried about finances or methods of child raising, they can relax and take more joy in the little ones.

"I left Ramona's house feeling a little better, but still wishing it was all a bad dream. I even half-hoped this one would miscarry like some of the others before."

Reflection and Prayer

Only those who are parents know all the sacrifices involved in pregnancy, infant care, and the rearing of children. Parenting a large family means twenty-four-hour availability, what with feedings every few hours, older children sick at night, incessant requests for water and juice, driving kids to activities, and late hours waiting up for older teens.

Besides other parents, however, there is one Other who understands. He is God, the very One whose personal intervention is necessary for the creation of the individual soul of your baby.

The evil one can make the words "one more baby" sound like just another animal in a litter. But as they embrace this new life and accept their new charge from the Lord, mothers and fathers become aware of the unique personhood of this irreplaceable and infinitely lovable member of the family.

If you face this situation, try praying this way:

"Dear Mother Mary, as this baby grows heavy in my womb, I offer the burden for the needs of everyone in our family, and also for those women who are seriously considering abortion. They feel they cannot face the sacrifices I have been given the grace to make through Christ, our Lord. Help them right now."

∼ *Scripture for Meditation* ∼

Shall Sarah, who is ninety years old, bear a child?

GENESIS 17:17

Elizabeth was barren, and both were advanced in years.... The angel said to him, "Do not be afraid, Zechariah, for your prayer is heard, and your wife Elizabeth will bear you a son, and you shall call his name John."

LUKE 1:7, 13

Whoever gives you a cup of water to drink because you bear the name of Christ, will by no means lose his reward.

MARK 9:41

My Daughter Is Pregnant But Not Married!

Thou didst knit me together in my mother's womb.

PSALM 139:13

"It's hard to believe Kathy would do this to us. We're pro-life activists. Every day of her life she heard about unmarried pregnant teens and how sad that they didn't try for chastity.

"I heard the news from my wife, because Kathy's afraid to tell me. She's sixteen. It happened with the first boy she's ever dated, also a 'good' Catholic!

"Of course we'll help her keep the baby or give him or her up for adoption if that seems the wisest course. Maybe she won't want to be at home. Then she could stay at one of those wonderful places for unmarried pregnant teens. I'm sure, with us as her family, she's not thinking of abortion, but I still can't stand knowing my own daughter would be that stupid and weak."

Reflection and Prayer

Parents who have worked for pro-life causes sometimes act as if having the right ideas is enough to overcome the temptations to premarital sex that most teens face. We know each person has free will. But when it comes to our own children, we sometimes imagine we can program them a certain way, and all will be well. Yet choosing virtue over sin takes more than the right ideas and education.

Pope John Paul II in his book *Love and Responsibility* wrote about the strong physical urges that contribute to feelings of lust in boys and men. He claims that for most girls and women, even stronger is a desire to be in love and to feel wanted by boys and men. Without a strong understanding and commitment to chastity and praying for grace before, during, and after encounters with the opposite sex, sin is likely to take place.

It is also absolutely necessary for men and women of any age to avoid near occasions of sin. For teens, that means avoiding unsupervised dating or parties. Perhaps the idea of chaperones, still in place in some more traditional societies, is not so stupid!

As the protective father of a pregnant teen you may feel you have failed. Don't you think God the Father was disappointed that David, the son he had showered with graces, yet fell into sin? You may also feel angry at your daughter for shaming you, even angrier at her boyfriend for being one of the immediate causes of the problem. Even though such feelings are natural, you need to bring them to Jesus and let him help you to heal.

You also owe it to your grandchild to emanate positive feelings toward him or her. Since God did allow this baby to be conceived and knit together in your daughter's womb, your response needs to be joy in the baby, even while you grieve the circumstances. Don't be so immersed in your own emotions that you can't give your daughter compassionate love and objective advice about her alternatives. This may be the time in her life she needs you the most.

Before times spent with your daughter, you might pray something like this:

"Lord, it was not wrong of me to hope that my children be chaste before marriage. You put that love for purity in my heart. Help me not to judge my daughter harshly at this time of vulnerability. May your fatherly love for her be mirrored in my doubled affection so that she feels secure. Let her be confident that you await her in sacramental confession so that she may have the grace to live your way of love better in the future."

～Scripture for Meditation～

It happened, late one afternoon, when David arose from his couch ... that he saw from the roof a woman bathing; and the woman was very beautiful.... So David sent messengers, and took her; and she came to him, and he lay with her. Then she returned to her house. And the woman conceived; and she sent and told David, "I am with child."

2 SAMUEL 11:2-5

Love covers a multitude of sins.

1 PETER 4:8

Let him who is without sin among you be the first to throw a stone.

JOHN 8:7

Two

Carry Me, Jesus, I'm So Tired

Come to me, all who labor and are heavy laden, and I will give you rest.

MATTHEW 11:28

When the phrase "chronic fatigue syndrome" first became popular, many immediately identified with the problem even without having the medical condition. Sometimes life is so difficult, and the burdens so heavy, that there seems to be no end in sight. Advice about lightening the load rings hollow.

If you look at the words of Jesus from the Gospel of Matthew cited above, you might wonder whether feeling tired and weary all the time is what he wants for you. After doctors have ruled out severe medical reasons for exhaustion, they will usually talk about stress-related fatigue. The sections to follow will take a look at various reasons for feeling tired: physical, emotional, and spiritual. (Financial stress will be discussed in chapter three.)

I'm So Tired I Could Drop!

For I will satisfy the weary soul, and every languishing soul I will replenish.

JEREMIAH 31:25

"When we had new babies every few years and I was up all night helping my wife and then working all day, I was tired all the time. But now, when most of the children have left and my job is routine, I am amazed at how exhausted I still feel. I can hardly drag myself out of bed in the morning, and I've started going to bed at 9:30 P.M.

"Our family doctor checked me out and didn't find anything wrong. He asked if I was happy with my life. 'Come on, Doc,' I said, 'you've lived long enough to know that no one lives happily ever after except when they've left this earth for heaven.'

"His response challenged me: 'It's true that life is full of crosses, but I'm talking about something else. When you savor the good in your life and have a balance of work, exercise, and fun, you experience a certain contentment.'

"The doctor suggested that I try a plan for six months that worked with other patients of my type. 'Schedule in one activity you enjoy every day,' he said. 'Before bed, recall everything good that happened that day in detail and thank God for it. Any time you feel fatigued or groggy, get up and move around, if only to walk around the block or get a drink of water. Do at least twenty minutes of hard exercise every other day.'

32

"Thank God, it worked. I couldn't believe how much less tired I felt following his routine. Now I don't have to think about it; I just naturally choose to enjoy what I can instead of grumbling about my frustrations all the time."

Reflection and Prayer

St. Francis of Assisi spoke of his body as "Brother Ass" and admitted that he treated it too harshly. Few Catholics would consider imitating the austerities of that wild and wonderful saint. However, many of us sin against our bodies by neglect.

Spiritual writers have a name for acting, in one way or the other, as if the body doesn't count. It is called "angelism." They call it that because angels are not essentially embodiments; they only appear in bodily form for our sake.

For humans to ignore the body can be prideful. By concentrating on mental work and otherwise lolling about, you can be acting as if, like an angel, you only have an intellect, will, and heart, without a body to take care of and refresh.

Another spiritual malady, rarely mentioned, comes when you think that you get merit only from bearing crosses. Many times such a philosophy of life can lead to a saggy, complaining disposition. You do please God greatly when bearing crosses out of love. Still, God is disappointed when you are so tired that you fail to enjoy the delights he is giving you as a relief. Wise spiritual directors tell zealous but burdened Catholics that they need to give themselves sufficient joyful recreation and rest precisely so that they don't burn out constantly working and helping.

~ *Scripture for Meditation* ~

The battle image in this passage from Deuteronomy can help you see that when you are too tired, you make an opening for the devil to tempt you to discouragement and other negative states:

Remember ... how he attacked you on the way, when you were faint and weary.

DEUTERONOMY 25:17-18

Woe is me! for the Lord has added sorrow to my pain; I am weary with my groaning, and I find no rest.

JEREMIAH 45:3

My yoke is easy, and my burden is light.

MATTHEW 11:30

Wait, Wait, Wait! Our Failure to Conceive a Child Is Unbearably Sad

I am weary with my crying; my throat is parched. My eyes grow dim with waiting for my God.

PSALM 69:3

"'Every month when my period comes again I go through dark depression,' I confessed. 'I've talked about it with my gynecologist, my mother, my sister (who has seven children), my priest, but nothing helps much. Fr. Paul said that maybe you could help.'

"I was talking to a pro-life counselor who was also a doctor. Dr. Reilly told me that she had quite a number of visits from women who have trouble conceiving. They usually come to her because they are interested in adopting children who might otherwise be aborted.

"I confided that I did realize that having a baby is not a right, but a gift from God. Just the same, each time we try something different to get pregnant and it doesn't work, I feel upset with God. Why us? Why couldn't he distribute babies more equally? All these couples with more than they want, and we get none!

"'Have you considered adoption?' the doctor asked me.

"'I'd like to do it, but my husband has these ideas about bad genes and crazed birth couples looking for their kid years afterwards.'

"'Tell me the methods you've tried so far, and I'll see whether you've missed something. In the meantime, why don't you pray for a month together with your husband to be open to whatever God wants for you?'"

Reflection and Prayer

The bewailing of barrenness is no new thing, as testified by the biblical stories of Sarah, Rachel, Hannah, and Elizabeth. It seems a nearly universal desire that married couples want a child to come from their sexual union.

Still, there is great goodness in adopting children, being a foster parent, or being a parental figure to other young people in the family or society. We have a great fatherly saint to prove it: St. Joseph! Yet the failure to conceive a child biologically is a terrible cross for many would-be parents.

Why God opens or shuts the womb is a mystery. Some women become pregnant at the least probable times. Others who work hard to pinpoint the day of greatest fertility never conceive. Quite a number of couples become pregnant after making the decision for adoption.

From the spiritual perspective, it is important to discern, perhaps with the help of a spiritual director, whether you and your spouse believe that you have a vocation to parenting. If you believe you do, then it would seem distrustful of God to be opposed to adoption or foster parenting. The Old Testament offers examples of adoption, and St. Paul likes to call us adopted children of God (see Gal 4:4-7). The joy of parents who have waited long and then conceived, and the joy of parents who receive in their arms the baby they wanted to adopt, seems pretty comparable!

~ *Scripture for Meditation* ~

The Lord said to Abraham, "Why did Sarah laugh, and say, 'Shall I indeed bear a child, now that I am old?' Is anything too hard for the Lord?"

GENESIS 18:13

When the Lord saw that Leah was hated, he opened her womb; but Rachel was barren.... When Rachel saw that she bore Jacob no children, she envied her sister; and she said to Jacob, "Give me children, or I shall die!" ... Then God remembered Rachel, and God hearkened to her and opened her womb.

GENESIS 29:31; 30:1, 22

[Mordecai] had brought up Hadassah, that is Esther, the daughter of his uncle,... and when her father and her mother died, Mordecai adopted her as his own daughter.

ESTHER 2:7

But they had no child, because Elizabeth was barren, and both were advanced in years.... But the angel said to him, "Do not be afraid, Zechariah, for your prayer is heard, and your wife Elizabeth will bear you a son."

LUKE 1:7, 13

And when [Moses] was exposed, Pharaoh's daughter adopted him and brought him up as her own son.

ACTS 7:21

Guilt Over Past Sins Is a Heavy Burden

It was not that this man sinned, or his parents, but that the works of God might be made manifest in him.

JOHN 9:3

"I can't get that memory out of my head. When I was twenty-four and my little brother was seventeen, he stole my car keys and went on a spree with his friends. I really gave it to him when he got back.

"'You nerd!' I shouted. 'If you ever take my car again without asking, I'll smash your head in!' The next day he was found with his head smashed in from a car accident caused by a buddy of his.

"I went to confession before the funeral. The priest said I was being too hard on myself. 'Threatening someone in anger who has done you a wrong is not a loving act, but it's understandable under those circumstances and certainly had nothing to do with your brother's death. You told me your brother was a good boy, even if a daredevil. Your brother is now in the loving arms of Jesus. Ask him to forgive you from where he is now.'

"I know in my head that I wasn't to blame, but I can't stand to think those were the last words my brother heard from me before he died. Sometimes I even wish I had died instead."

Reflection and Prayer

Why do you sometimes feel worse about a particular sin you've confessed long ago, and sometimes ignore worse sins of the present?

There's a story about a monk on his deathbed. The brother who tended him was surprised that he didn't ask the others in the order for forgiveness, which was the usual custom. Instead this dying monk was radiant with joy.

When asked about his behavior, the monk replied: "I have always forgiven everyone immediately, and I have always confessed every sin immediately and asked forgiveness of those I hurt. Jesus says he will forgive us our trespasses as we forgive those who trespass against us, so I have no fear."

Jesus instituted the sacrament of reconciliation to bring repentant sinners to peace. He doesn't want you to be burdened by memories of past sins as long as you've confessed them. He wants you to be like a child whose wailing is cut off mid-scream if something good comes along.

Inner turmoil over past mistakes or sins indicates lack of trust in Jesus. He knows the weaknesses of our fallen nature. He wants to transform the energy and time you put into self-flagellation into resolute desire to call on his grace so that you can be better, precisely in the area of the shameful sin that haunts you.

Refusal to accept forgiveness from God can have other bad consequences. After all, if you believe you can't be forgiven, how well do you forgive others? There were saints who were murderers but who lived to repent and become holy: St. Paul was the first.

A prayer you might say when bad memories of the past assail you is this:

"Here I am, Jesus, Savior. You know everything I have ever done wrong. I give you my painful memories. I accept that pain as part of my punishment.

"I place in your heart anyone who was victimized by my sins. We are yours. Let me not omit the loving deeds you want of me today through preoccupation with bad ones of the past."

∼ *Scripture for Meditation* ∼

He heals the brokenhearted, and binds up their wounds.

PSALM 147:3

May the God of peace himself sanctify you wholly;... He who calls you is faithful, and he will do it.

1 THESSALONIANS 5:23-24

Love covers a multitude of sins.

1 PETER 4:8

I Feel Overwhelmed by Life Itself!

There [after death] the weary are at rest.

JOB 3:17

"I guess this is what it means to be 'over the hill.' Since my fiftieth birthday I feel as if all that's left for me are crosses, more and more each year. Maybe it's being in what someone called 'the sandwich generation.' My age group is sandwiched between worries about the youngest ones in our family, now teenagers still at home, and also taking care of our elderly parents and relatives. It doesn't help that my husband left a few years ago to marry a younger woman.

" 'Cut down,' some people say. 'Get more rest.' But it's not that I'm too busy. Everything does fit into a normal day if there are no emergencies. I sleep eight hours a night. Maybe it's what's called bone-weariness. It seems that life itself is too much: too much fuss, too much conflict, too much sadness, too much depression, too much tragedy on the news, too much noise.

"I love to go to Mass in the morning during the week and feel the silence and peace. But at least halfway through it I'm distracted by the list in my head of what has to be done, or flashing images of the people I love who seem so unhappy.

"I realize that true peace will come in heaven; God willing, I'll get there. But shouldn't life itself be a little easier?"

Reflection and Prayer

Weariness can actually be a good thing. It can indicate a life full of charitable sacrifice. When you feel tired after a day of hard but successful work, it is not a reason for despair, but for satisfaction.

Nevertheless, when you feel overwhelmed with life itself, the "gray tone" of day-to-day living is different from meritorious fatigue. Such a state of mind used to be called in Latin *taedium vitae*—the "tedium of life."

You might see such a blah feeling of life as a sign that a change is needed. Having good vacation times, a real Sabbath, could help a lot. But you need as well to consider what is going on inside. A lot of your activities may have become too routine. Perhaps they are no longer motivated by conscious love of God and neighbor, but more by habit.

When such feelings are dominant, it can be good to take a day off at a retreat house or in some beautiful natural setting. Perhaps God might tell you something like this: "You are a good and worthy servant. If you died tomorrow, your guardian angel would have a long enough list of good deeds to defend you against damnation. You may not need to do a single thing more just to avoid hell. Rest in that thought."

Next, the Holy Spirit might show you, one by one, the persons you help on a regular basis. Jesus might ask you to make a fresh choice; for instance: "Here is your aunt in the convalescent home. All week long she waits for your visit. Don't you want to continue giving her that joy?" He might show you some other ministry that could be dropped since there are others who can do it better or more easily.

One antidote to low feelings may be to accompany your chores with Christian music. When the beauty of the words and melodies lifts your spirits, you overcome inertia and often perform your works with greater love. Talking to Jesus throughout the day about your work is a common characteristic of the saints. He'd be glad to keep you company if you really wanted him to!

A prayer for those overwhelmed by life itself:

"Let me consider how you, the Son of God, living in ecstasy in heaven, were yet willing to come down to our sinful world and spend so many years engaging in tasks good in themselves but hardly exciting. Instead of sagging under these burdens, your interior life of union with your Father filled these tasks with love.

"Please send the Holy Spirit to buoy me up under my load. Like Mother Teresa may I be willing to do little things with great love. Keep me from despair. Open me to see the gifts you want to give me day by day so that I may radiate hope."

∼ *Scripture for Meditation* ∼

Like a swallow or a crane I clamor, I moan like a dove. My eyes are weary with looking upward. O Lord, I am oppressed; be thou my security!... All my sleep has fled because of the bitterness of my soul.

ISAIAH 38:14-15

I will come upon him [David] while he is weary and discouraged, and throw him into a panic; and all the people who are with him will flee.

2 SAMUEL 17:2

I know you are enduring patiently and bearing up for my name's sake, and you have not grown weary. But I have this against you, that you have abandoned the love you had at first.

REVELATION 2:3-4

There's Never Enough Time in the Day for All I Have to Do!

With a yoke on our necks we are hard driven; we are weary, we are given no rest.

LAMENTATIONS 5:5

"I've just about had it. My life seems like a modern form of slavery. When my company offered a workshop on time management, I signed up. We were asked to write down our schedules. Here was mine for weekdays.

"Morning:

"6:00—Get up.

"6:45—Begin commute in heavy traffic, listening to the business news.

"8:00—At the desk.

"12:00 noon—Lunch, usually with other managers where we talk shop.

"Afternoon:

"1:00—At the desk.

"5:00—If overtime not needed at office, commute home in heavy traffic listening to international news.

"Evening:

"6:00—Arrive home and help my wife with dinner and kids.

"7:00—Carpooling to sports and music with the kids.

"8:00—Work at home on office work I brought with me.

"9:00—Chauffeur kids back from their activities.

"9:30—TV news and bed.

"My list for weekends was a little better, but it included going to kids' sports competitions, yard work in summer, snow clearing in winter, trips to the discount stores to stock up on staples, and Sunday Mass.

"The director of the workshop asked us also to compute the time we would say was totally relaxing for us. For me that amounted to about five hours a week max. Then came advice about how to drop things: 'Make your life more enjoyable and others will enjoy it more, too.'

"I'm confused. It doesn't seem right to gain leisure time at the expense of everyone else's needs. For starters, I don't think the family would go for living poor just so I could work at some easy job with no overtime."

Reflection and Prayer

Humorous sayings about being too busy abound: "Guess what? On the day you die, there will still be something left to do on your desk!" Another favorite goes like this: "If you're too busy to pray, you're too busy!" Then there's the cartoon that shows a harried-looking older man standing at his desk. He is on the phone. The caption reads: "How about never? Would that be a good time for you?"

The fictional narrative for this topic doesn't get into how disgruntled, irritable, and generally hard to live with most men and women are who try to "do it all." All your commitments may be for the sake of love, but sometimes there is little love in each activity because you're exhausted!

If you have a heavy schedule, you may be one of those Christians who think that you don't have time to pray more. A morning offering and nightly examination of conscience might be all you think you can squeeze in on a daily basis. It may be difficult, if not impossible, to be liberated from the feeling that you have to do it all till you drop dead, without more time with your Creator.

There can be an element of pride, sometimes called *grandiosity,* in trying to do more than can be humanly balanced, as if by inordinate sacrifices you can ensure the happiness of your family. Humility can sometimes require getting more help from others. Even Moses, the great leader of the Jewish people, needed support. One time when he wearied of holding his hands up in prayer during a battle, Aaron and Hur came alongside him and held them up for him (see Ex 17:12).

It is not unusual these days to find the earliest Mass in a parish each morning attended by scores of people on their way to work. They know that they need God's help every day! Even if most of your prayer is in your car during the commute, that is better than pretending you have everything under control and don't need God except in emergencies.

During your prayer time throughout the next month, you might talk to God about your deepest values and goals. You could ask the whole family to do the same. At family meetings you could begin with prayer to help members feel secure enough to avoid defensiveness. Then you could share about how you see your schedules in relation to those values and goals.

Some families have each child pick out one and only one favorite outside activity to take part in. Others sacrifice living in the perfect neighborhood to reside, instead, in a reasonably safe area nearer the main breadwinner's job to reduce commute time. In response to a mid-life crisis, sometimes husband or wife may alter their career trajectories for the purpose of working at something more fulfilling with a less taxing schedule.

A prayer for families about scheduling could be this:

"Jesus, Mary, and Joseph, we know you love our family. We picture you in Nazareth being occupied with many works of love, of a physical or spiritual nature. But we don't imagine you are frantic and miserable doing that work. Please help us see what is really important, what leads to our salvation and sanctification, and what needs to be changed so that we can be a happier and holier family."

∼Scripture for Meditation ∼

But Moses' hands grew weary; so they took a stone and put it under him, and he sat upon it, and Aaron and Hur held up his hands, one on one side, the other on the other side; so his hands were steady until the going down of the sun.

Exodus 17:12

Yet you did not call upon me, O Jacob; but you have been weary of me, O Israel!

Isaiah 43:22

Martha, Martha, you are anxious and troubled about many things; one thing is needful.

Luke 10:41-42

My Life Has Become So Boring

O God, thou art my God, I seek thee, my soul thirsts for thee; my flesh faints for thee, as in a dry and weary land where no water is.... I will lift up my hands and call on thy name.

PSALM 63:1, 4

"I won't forget that day, a year ago, when I stood on the street in front of our house watching my daughter and her children get in the car and go. She was the last of our five children to leave home. My husband is sixty. He has five years to go before retiring on pension and Social Security. All our grown children have jobs in other states. So now it's just 'the rooster and the hen,' as I've heard say.

"For a few weeks it felt good to realize all I had to do was shop, cook, and clean. With just the two of us, that doesn't amount to more than about four hours a day. I started going to daily Mass and rosary with my neighbor. I love that.

"When I get back to my own four walls, I put the breakfast dishes into the dishwasher. Then I tackle different chores such as sorting out clothing from the dryer or, big thrill, washing the kitchen floor. By now huge jobs such as cleaning out the basement and the attic are all done. So there's nothing much to do between 11:00 A.M. and 6:00 P.M. when George comes back.

"A trivial problem? Certainly, if you compare it to taking care of a father with Alzheimer's as my neighbor does. Still, some days I sit in my recliner and weep from the loneliness of missing my children and the emptiness in my life."

Reflection and Prayer

"The empty nest" well describes the plight of the woman who gave herself totally to the family and then finds herself alone in her home most of the day. The fear of this time can haunt a middle-aged person long before the actual last child leaves.

Nevertheless, there is always plenty of work to do, volunteer or paid, in the community and in the church. So why wouldn't you find many important things to do each day, instead of sitting at home?

If you are like some older women, you prefer being in the cozy, familiar environment of your own home to being out among relative strangers. You may also feel insecure about your skills. The phrase "I'm just a housewife" speaks poignantly of the low self-esteem of some women—despite the fact that raising a family is one of the hardest jobs in the world, requiring many virtues and talents few career women can boast of.

Transformation in Christ, a twentieth-century classic on spirituality by Dietrich von Hildebrand, begins with a chapter entitled "The Readiness to Change." The author observes that sometimes you don't really want to make the changes that are necessary for growth. Coming into a new period in your life especially requires a readiness to change.

God can help you move out of a comfortable but stagnant lifestyle by a process that could be likened to weaning. In the past, breastfeeding mothers who wanted to wean their children used to blacken the breast with a sticky, unpleasant-smelling substance. Disgusted, the baby was more willing to move from milk to other liquids.

In a similar way, when God wants to move us into change, he sometimes blackens our present conditions. Because we are so unhappy, we are more open to new people and new God-inspired works of love.

Perhaps you need to pray something like this:

"I believe, dear God, that you have a plan for my life. I know you don't want me to spend my time longing for the past. Of all those in my environment who need help, please show me the ones I can best serve. Give me confidence to move forward. Give me the willingness to endure the crosses, big and small, of the new ministries you would have me give myself to."

⁓ Scripture for Meditation ⁓

Have you not known? Have you not heard? The Lord is the everlasting God, the Creator of the ends of the earth. He does not faint or grow weary, his understanding is unsearchable. He gives power to the faint, and to him who has no might he increases strength.... They who wait for the Lord shall renew their strength, they shall mount up with wings like eagles, they shall run and not be weary, they shall walk and not faint.

ISAIAH 40:28-31

And let us not grow weary in well-doing, for in due season we shall reap, if we do not lose heart.

GALATIANS 6:9

I came that they may have life, and have it abundantly.

JOHN 10:10

Three

Help, God, I Need You to Provide!

The Lord is my shepherd, I shall not want.

PSALM 23:1

Some Christians go through life with few if any financial problems. They seem to have been born in the "green pastures" of Psalm 23. Perhaps they have inherited wealth. Most often they have worked at challenging jobs that others find hard to stick with.

Such relative affluence can be part of God's providence, especially when those who are so blessed share generously with the poor. Those with adequate incomes should be grateful to be free of the cross of severe money worries.

Of the millions of Christians throughout the centuries since Jesus walked our earth, probably most have suffered at some time from real poverty, financial insecurity, debt, or fear of these. If you are one of those now, or you might be in the future, read on to avoid being overwhelmed. Jesus wants to meet you in these problems.

I Hate Worrying About Money All the Time!

What woman, having ten silver coins, if she loses one coin, does not light a lamp and sweep the house and seek diligently until she finds it?

LUKE 15:8

"I came from a poor family. My parents were worried about money most of the time. We children had to do without lots of the things my classmates took for granted.

"We never ate out at any place better than 'the Golden Arches,' my father's funny name for McDonald's. Except for the oldest boy and girl, we all wore hand-me-downs. No vacations for us. I envied those with more and vowed to work as hard as I could, never to be poor when I grew up.

"During high school I worked in my spare time at the supermarket. When I graduated, I worked at the same chain full time and went to community college at night. When we got married, my wife was working. We figured we could put in day care any babies that came along. Everyone else was doing it.

"My wife and I agreed on this plan until our first, little Joey, was born. We had a big mortgage to pay on our house, but Allie insisted she wanted to stay home and be with our son.

"So now we're living a lot like I did as a kid, watching the money all the time. Sometimes I feel overwhelmed, thinking how we could lose our home if any major repairs were needed. We'd be wiped out."

Reflection and Prayer

Since it is unlikely that those who are truly destitute would use their money to buy a book such as this, the reflections here are about what could be called "relative poverty." Ironically, what we in the United States consider to be living poor would seem like miraculous provision to many people in other countries. Just the same, given the lifestyle of many middle-income people, not being able to have everything you want and worrying about unexpected emergencies can be very difficult.

To avoid anxiety and envy, you need to see life in terms of God's values, not the world's. Success in the kingdom of God is to be a loving person, not to have lots of things. When you come to your final judgment, wouldn't you be surprised if God asked you about the make of your car instead of about the children you loved?

"But," you might retort, "the house and car aren't luxuries. They're necessities. I'm a family man. I don't think God wants me to live like St. Francis of Assisi. So I have to worry about supporting the family through the setbacks that can't be avoided."

A prayer that fits such circumstances would be this:

"Thank you, God, for all that we have, especially you. Remind me to look around at my blessings and thank you for them one by one each day. Teach me to be happy with what you have given me.

"The Holy Spirit teaches us through the Church to live simply. Let me see my treasure in those I love. When I feel anxious about expenses, let me give my fears to you, trusting that you will provide not so much what we want as what we need. Please keep what we really need from breaking down!"

∼ Scripture for Meditation ∼

You shall remember the Lord your God, for it is he who gives you power to get wealth.

DEUTERONOMY 8:18

"See the man who would not make God his refuge, but trusted in the abundance of his riches, and sought refuge in his wealth!" But I am like a green olive tree in the house of God. I trust in the steadfast love of God for ever and ever.

PSALM 52:7-8

Give us this day our daily bread.

MATTHEW 6:11

When Will We Ever Be Free of Debt?

In everything a prudent man acts with knowledge.

PROVERBS 13:16

"When Phil and I decided to get married right after college, we knew we would have financial problems. His debt from college loans amounted to $15,000, and mine was $25,000!

"We prayed about it. It didn't seem as if God would want us to postpone getting married for the five years it might take to pay off those loans by living separately with our own families. Since we both wanted to devote ourselves to Church work, we knew the salaries wouldn't be that great, but we figured we'd live simply in a rented apartment and gradually clear our debt.

"The first year was OK. We were paying off the debt slowly but surely and just about making it on our combined low salaries from the high school where we were teaching. When I got pregnant, the problems really hit us.

"Even though medical insurance paid our doctor and hospital, I wanted to be an at-home mother. That meant half the income we were used to having. We decided to borrow money from my parents to get through the baby's first year, and then see what to do next.

"After a year of struggling along, we realized that Phil would have to forget about Church work. He got a job with a good salary in the business world. His folks gave us a down payment for a small house.

We renegotiated our payment plans on the college loans with a lower monthly payment, but with more years of debt than before.

"Sometimes our debt feels almost like a member of the family—a hated one! A third of Phil's salary goes to the debt. The rest barely pays for all our necessities."

Reflection and Prayer

Debt has become a major problem for many middle-class Christians. Some get so overwhelmed by their debt that they declare bankruptcy, with all the penalties of loss of credit. Even those who do not go that far wonder whether payment of debt is a moral obligation.

There are too many variations between economies worldwide for moral theologians to lay down strict rules about incurring and paying off debt. But in general, here are some principles.

Forgiving the debts of others is a virtue (see Ez 18:7). The practice is so noble as to be used by Jesus as an analogy for your forgiveness of the sins of others and God's forgiveness of your sins (see Mt 18:21-35). Nonetheless, barring an unexpected reprieve, you are obligated to fulfill promises and contracts, including paying debts (see the *Catechism of the Catholic Church,* 2410-2411).

No matter how common and how good your motives, living beyond your means is imprudent. Accumulating debt can sometimes result from subtle forms of pride. For example, why make it a necessity to finish college in four years no matter how much debt is racked up?

Concerns about status could also be involved. It is a sign of affluence for your parents to be able to exempt you from the burden of being a full-time wage earner like most of the rest of humanity. Might it be more prudent to go to college slowly, taking off every other year to earn the tuition and expenses for the next one? Or to get married partway through and then slowly work for a degree, course by course, as finances allow?

Many people consider owning a house to be a right rather than a gift. As a result they will buy a house before they can afford it, without considering how much less it would cost to buy a mobile home or rent an apartment.

Having made imprudent decisions, often with good motives, what are you to do when the consequences seem overwhelming? Some parishes have volunteer businessmen and women offering free financial advice to those struggling with financial woes. Even if they are not professional advisors, they may be able to help you. Your priest or parish counselor may know of such persons.

In the meantime, here is a prayer you could say:

"Dear God, thank you for the many benefits I have enjoyed in my life so far. I am grateful for them even if they have a negative side. In the future I want to plan my life in a more prudent way.

"Please send the Holy Spirit and my guardian angel to keep me from more unwise decisions. If we have to scale down, please heal me and my family from any fears attached to not looking affluent. Never let me choose affluence over having the children God intends for us."

∼ *Scripture for Meditation* ∼

[The proverbs in Scripture have been given to us] that prudence may be given to the simple.

PROVERBS 1:4

O simple ones, learn prudence; O foolish men, pay attention.

PROVERBS 8:5

A man of discretion is patient.

PROVERBS 14:17

Therefore the kingdom of heaven may be compared to a king who wished to settle accounts with his servants. When he began the reckoning, one was brought to him who owed him ten thousand talents [about $10,000]; and as he could not pay, his lord ordered him to be sold, with his wife and children and all that he had, and payment to be made.

MATTHEW 18:23-25

What Job Should I Take?

Do not be conformed to this world but be transformed by the renewal of your mind, that you may prove what is the will of God, what is good and acceptable and perfect.

ROMANS 12:2

"For years I've dreamed of getting out of secular TV, with all its moral compromises, to work for a Catholic station. Now I have an offer, but I'm torn. The salary would be half what I am getting now. We'd have to move from the state where most of our family members still live, to go to a state where we don't know anyone.

"I really feel called by God to take the new position, but my wife hates the idea. She's not as religious as I am. She thinks that the people who run the Catholic TV station are old-fashioned fanatics.

"She also collects stories of people who go into Church work only to become disillusioned. Such Catholics idealistically assume that if everyone is a true believer, there won't be other problems. But once in the new job, they wind up being miserable on half or less of their previous salaries.

"Part of the problem is my wife's shopping addiction. Even with my large salary and my wife's income from computer work at home, we're always on the edge because of credit card debt. Between weekly mall binges and major purchases such as new cars, giant home entertainment screens, and surprise cruises to celebrate my birthday, we're about $50,000 in the hole.

"No wonder she doesn't want to give me a chance to respond to God's new plan for our lives. I wish she'd let me follow gospel values. If she wants luxuries so much, let her pay for them with her own salary!"

Reflection and Prayer

It is not unusual at midlife or later for a couple with originally compatible values to experience conflict. This situation can be especially complicated when it involves a major change based on conversion to a more apostolic lifestyle. The zealous party has to bear in mind that when he or she got married, there was probably an implicit understanding that both spouses wanted everything their money could buy.

On the other hand, the Church teaches that all Catholics should live simply. Such a norm is usually feasible for singles and older couples if not for most families with children. Sessions with a spiritual director or a marriage counselor respected by both spouses could help them arrive at a compromise.

Involvement with a movement such as Marriage Encounter could bring both husband and wife to better ways to relate to each other as spouses and as brother and sister in Christ. Trying out a new way without burning bridges can also sometimes give space for unexpected insights.

Here is a prayer for discernment involving job changes:

"Come, Holy Spirit, we call upon the graces of the sacrament of marriage as we open ourselves to your will for our future employment and place of residence. Keep us from clinging, through inertia, to anything of the past that is not of your will. Keep us also from rushing toward a glittering prospect that may turn out to be frustrating.

"Let neither of us think only of our individual needs, but instead pray that every wholesome goal of the other may be fulfilled by this choice. Give us the security to believe that you will bring good out of the choice we make at this time. We trust in your love."

～ *Scripture for Meditation* ～

This text is not about marriage, but it fits our theme since it is often used in the marriage ceremony:

But Ruth said... "For where you go I will go, and where you lodge I will lodge;... and your God [will be] my God; where you die I will die, and there will I be buried."

RUTH 1:16-17

An angel of the Lord appeared to Joseph in a dream and said, "Rise, take the child and his mother, and flee to Egypt, and remain there till I tell you."

MATTHEW 2:13

You cannot serve God and mammon.

MATTHEW 6:24

It's So Hard Being a Single Parent!

What troubles you, Hagar? Fear not; for God has heard the voice of the lad where he is. Arise, lift up the lad, and hold him fast with your hand.

GENESIS 21:17-18

"The divorce was my idea. My husband's drinking problem was getting worse and worse to the point where he was passing out every night. He refused to go to a twelve-step program or any other kind of treatment since he was in denial.

"It's not just that it was hurting me; I didn't want it to hurt the kids or to give them a bad example, especially since they were soon to be teenagers. My priest knows my husband well. After all else failed, he said that under the circumstances getting a divorce would be an option.

"I was satisfied with the legal settlement at the time, but now that my boys are older, it's getting rough. I wake up in the night worrying about their future.

"We always planned that they'd go to college. But my husband remarried outside the Church, and now with keeping up two households, the best we could do for the boys would be junior college. They'd have to work and go at night so they could make car payments on a second car.

"Sometimes it feels as if God just doesn't love us. It's so complicated to find solutions to problems that two-parent families can solve so much more easily."

Reflection and Prayer

Many are the problems of single parents. Financial difficulties are not the least. It is not so much that single parents are greedy for luxuries, but that they naturally want for their children what they expected to have on full double incomes.

If you feel overwhelmed in trying to make ends meet, consider the plight of Hagar, the mother of Ishmael, Abraham's son, sent off to the desert. Her son was about to die before God intervened miraculously to save mother and child and to predict a great future for them as well.

Even if you are not a widow, you might want to read about saintly widows with heavy problems raising older children, such as St. Rita of Cascia and St. Elizabeth Ann Seton. As a single parent you need to be especially close to the Holy Family so that they can help you discern how to get through life day by day.

You will want to engage in spiritual warfare against the demons of bitterness and discouragement. You need to believe that God has a loving plan for you, each of your children, and for your former spouse as well. When you feel the whole world is on your shoulders, ask for the grace to see the humor in daily life. Ask for the trust that will make it possible to become a sign of Christian joy.

A prayer to the Holy Family:

"I am coming to you, Jesus, Mary, and Joseph, with hope that you will stay close to our little family in our troubles. Sometimes we feel so angry that our divorce means so many sacrifices for us now. Help us to value forgiveness as a crucial way to become the holy women and men you want us to become.

"Can you give us some extra graces during this difficult time? Help us to put our trust in you day by day and rejoice in every good gift you choose to give us."

∼ *Scripture for Meditation* ∼

But even the hairs of your head are all numbered. Fear not, therefore; you are of more value than many sparrows.

MATTHEW 10:30-31

Rejoice in the Lord, always; again I will say, Rejoice.

PHILIPPIANS 4:4

Every good endowment and every perfect gift is from above, coming down from the Father of lights.

JAMES 1:17

I Don't Want to Be a Burden!

For salvation is nearer to us now than when we first believed.

ROMANS 13:11

"All my life I saved. I wanted to be sure I could live comfortably at my own expense in my old age. When the stock market took a dip, I found that I not only lost a lot on certain specific investments, but my pension, based on the market, also went down. My income is now half what I thought it would be.

"Before my wife died we took out an equity loan on our house so we could help one of our daughters with a down payment for her first house. So when I sold the house, I didn't get any profit out of it.

"Last year I had a stroke. Afterwards I had to move into my daughter's house so there'd be someone around to help me out. My teenage grandson did as much as he could after school when my daughter was at work. Now he's gone to college.

"The kids all pitched in to help me pay for an attendant. That costs almost $100 a day, much more than I can afford on my Social Security and reduced pension. I am so upset at being such a burden that I pray to die soon.

"My daughter asked the parish priest if he could come over and hear my confession. She didn't think it was right for me to be praying to die. The priest asked if I were angry at God about the way things turned out.

"I don't really go with this idea of people being angry at God. It doesn't make sense. God didn't cause the stock market to crash. But after the priest explained more, I could see that somehow I haven't accepted that God would allow me to be shamed in this way, having to be a burden to my grown children."

Reflection and Prayer

How nice it would be if you were to die tranquilly in your sleep with thousands of dollars set aside for each of your children or relatives! It is hard to face the possibility and then the actuality of quite a different scenario for your last years on this earth. You simply can't control the future, and when life turns out differently from the way you planned it, you are inclined to wonder why. Yet such philosophical reflections about old age don't help too much when the disappointments and crosses seem unbearable.

In the next chapter you will learn more about meeting Christ in sickness and disability. For now, the emphasis will be on monetary difficulties that can go along with those crosses.

Enforced dependence can force the reevaluation of certain worldly notions that are more cultural than Christian. Is it really better to be an independent individual living alone, not needing anyone else except for occasional company? If adult children have money to spare, is it really better for them to spend it on luxuries than to help the parents who sacrificed so much for them when they were young? What brings a family closer to Jesus: relief that no one has any claim on their money, or gratitude for help in time of need? Couldn't it be part of God's providence for a large family to pitch in to help an incapacitated parent?

Such questions call to mind the famous poster with a beaming boy of about ten years old carrying on his back another little boy of about three. The caption read: "He's not heavy, he's my brother."

During the many hours you have to pray, these thoughts might be thematic:

"Dear Lord, you know how much I wanted to spare my children this burden. Thank you for their generosity of time and money. Please compensate them for it on earth or in eternity. Help me to reward them by not being touchy when they grow impatient about their sacrifices.

"Overcome my pride so that I can accept the humility of my present position in life. Keep me from futile thoughts and blame concerning the economic situation of my country. Let me treasure each moment of enjoying my children and grandchildren, the trees in the yard, the stars at night. I offer to you the sufferings of this period in my life so that one day everyone in my family may be reunited in heaven."

～ *Scripture for Meditation* ～

O that I might have my request, and that God would grant my desire; that it would please God to crush me, that he would let loose his hand and cut me off!... What is my strength, that I should wait? And what is my end, that I should be patient? Is my strength the strength of stones, or is my flesh bronze? In truth I have no help in me, and any resource is driven from me.

JOB 6:8-13

Only in the Lord ... are righteousness and strength; to him shall come and be ashamed, all who were incensed against him. In the Lord all the offspring of Israel shall triumph and glory.

ISAIAH 45:24-25

Bear one another's burdens, and so fulfil the law of Christ.

GALATIANS 6:2

Four

Lord, the One You Love Is Sick!

"Lord, if you will, you can make me clean." And he stretched out
his hand and touched him, saying, "I will; be clean." And imme-
diately his leprosy was cleansed.

MATTHEW 8:2-3

We will be addressing individually the various kinds of suffering caused by sickness and disability. But first, we need an overview of the various attitudes Christians may take toward physical suffering.

For many centuries most Catholics thought that the healing ministry was confined to Jesus, the intercession of Mary, and canonizable saints. Catholics tended to think of any illness or disability that did not go away with prayer and medical treatment as a cross to offer up in reparation for their own sins or for special intentions.

During the second half of the twentieth century came an upsurge of healings through the prayer of Christians of all states in life, sometimes through laying on of hands. Healings were especially prominent in groups claiming the charismatic gifts of the Holy Spirit. Since the Gospel quoted above says "if you will," we need to understand that Jesus still has the power to heal at any time "if he will."

Does it follow, then, that in the innumerable cases of health problems from the womb all the way to natural death, Jesus does *not* want to heal? This query is not solely of academic interest. To the afflicted and those who love them, it can become a burning question—sometimes destroying faith, sometimes opening new insight into the ways of God.

Suffering is a mystery. There is no way we can reason to a clear understanding of it. But one help is to distinguish between God's perfect will and his permissive will. God did not create pain and death as an essential part of the world. Scripture teaches that these realities came about as a consequence of original sin.

Mother Teresa of Calcutta once spoke of such suffering as part of the drama of life as we know it. God's perfect will was Eden. He could have wiped out the world after the sin of Adam and Eve. He permitted, instead, that we continue on to make free choices, crippled by defects of all kinds, in a world full of natural beauty but potential disaster. Given a foretaste of heaven by the joys of our lives; weaned from this world by pain; opened to love, human and divine; we can be prepared for a heaven greater than the original paradise we lost.

From this perspective, incurable disability and persistent sickness can be viewed and received as a cross permitted by God to purify us. Medical healing can bind us in gratitude to human professionals. Miracles can show us God's power and personal love.

The Christian understanding presented in response to the narratives to follow may not touch directly on the form of sickness or disability you are concerned with. Nevertheless, I hope you will be able to get comfort and understanding from the Holy Spirit in applying to your own case what is written here.

I'm So Afraid!

Perfect love casts out fear.

1 JOHN 4:18

"I'm a single woman of forty. All my life I've been afraid of illness and disability even though I, myself, am fairly healthy. My grandmother lived with us until her death. No one paid attention to her physical complaints. One day, her heart stopped beating and she died while we waited for the ambulance. My doctor said if she'd had surgery, she would have lived ten years longer!

"I think my grandmother's sudden death was the start of my chronic worry. Having a little niece with Down's Syndrome has also saddened me greatly. I watch myself and others closely, reading health magazines and trying to warn people before disaster strikes.

"When it's icy, I worry that people will slip and break their legs or hips. My father has asthma, and I'm always afraid allergic responses will trigger a fatal episode. A colleague at my office suddenly developed a brain tumor and died within the year. Someone said that if he had only gone to check out his fierce headaches, they would have gotten to him in time.

"I watch my teenage nephew smoking and tell him about the risks of lung cancer, with all the pain that disease would bring not only to him but to the children he will leave behind. So many foods are now considered to be dangerous, so I made up a special diet and stay away from restaurants and resorts where I can't control what is served.

"My friends laugh at me. They think I'm crazy with all these fears. I think they're the ones who live in a dream world. They act as if everything happens to strangers and never to themselves or those they love. My mother says I need to have more faith in God."

Reflection and Prayer

Religious philosophers explain that the quality known as *contingency* is part of the very nature of a created being. This is to say that only God is absolute, existing no matter what, while creatures may come into existence or pass away, depending on him for their existence. We humans cannot hold our bodily existence in a tight grip.

At any moment you can die of the slightest accidental occurrence, such as a car running over you on your own street. From one day to the next your body can move from seemingly perfect health to catastrophic disability. Given these realities, you could have a reason to be fearful every moment of your life.

Nevertheless, Pope John Paul II has pointed out how often Jesus addressed those he wanted to heal with these words: "Be not afraid!" In light of so many dangers, however, you might be tempted to respond, "How dare Jesus tell me not to be afraid!"

God does not blame you for feeling fear. He begs you, though, to run to him with your fears so that he can calm you.

Only when your prayer is as strong as your fear will you be able to understand that bodily life on earth is not the goal. If God allows a Down's Syndrome baby to be born, it is not an accident. Such a child, though handicapped in some ways, has great love to give.

When you pray as the psalmist did, expressing your emotions fully, your heart will be open to his comfort. Immersed in God's absolute goodness, you will be better able to look forward to heaven, not earth, as your home. God wants you to live in a healthy way and to pray for an end of sickness and disability. But he doesn't want you to value the body so much that your mind is focused more on its preservation than on your eternal goals.

You might well ask yourself: What does it mean if I have no time for daily Mass but use the same time for aerobics? What does it mean if I spend more time reading health magazines than reading God's Word?

A prayer to overcome fear:

"Dear Jesus, you did not promise us happiness on earth. You healed many sick and disabled people. Many others were left better for having known you and trusting that there would be an end to their pain in heaven.

"Please have the Holy Spirit remind me to bring my fears about physical suffering and handicap to you. Show me how to warn others of hazards in a peaceful manner, so that they know they are in your loving hands no matter what happens to them. May all those I have fears about find the best treatments possible for their ills."

∼ *Scripture for Meditation* ∼

Be not afraid.

LUKE 2:10

Do not fear those who kill the body, and after that have no more that they can do.... Fear him who, after he has killed, has power to cast into hell.

LUKE 12:4-5

We know that in everything God works for good with those who love him, who are called according to his purpose.

ROMANS 8:28

What Could It Be?

[She] had suffered much under many physicians, and had spent all that she had, and was no better but rather grew worse.

MARK 5:26

"Two years after I finished college with a business major, it began with what seemed like flu. I drank lots of orange juice for vitamin C and went to work at my dad's accounting firm anyhow. When I didn't get better after a few weeks, I went to the doctor.

"She couldn't find anything unusual. She suggested lots of rest. She said it could be stress-related. I started feeling weaker and sleepier, with intermittent fever and headaches. I stopped going to the office and stayed at home. The digestive problems increased.

"I was tested at a world-famous clinic. I checked with health food experts and was prayed over by healers. Pills, exercise treatments, counselors—nothing has helped. Most of all I feel totally bored and depressed now. How can I be cured if no one knows what the problem is?

"I'm a practicing Catholic. Since I had a good job and no debts, I was planning to surf the Catholic singles scene to look for a wife and start a family. Now I can't plan anything. I don't even know when I'll have the strength to get up regularly in the morning and go back to work. I plead with God to help me. He doesn't seem to be answering."

Reflection and Prayer

Contemporary religious writers often emphasize "living in the now" instead of being preoccupied with the future. There is truth in this admonition. In reality, in this present life, all we have is the now. The past is gone, and the future is not yet here.

Living in the now feels good when your now is full of pleasures. But what about when the now is empty and the future depends on healings that aren't forthcoming?

Times of uncertainty caused by undiagnosed but disabling illness call for a conversion of your whole person from an activist mentality to one of heroic interior trust. Between visits to doctors there will be nothing meaningful to do about your state but pray. Neck-and-neck with prayers for a diagnosis or a remission will have to be prayers of surrender to the God who made you and who alone can give you the hope you need to overcome despair.

Enforced idleness can be an opportunity for Scripture study, meditation, and contemplation of eternal truth. No less a hero than the founder of the Jesuit Order, St. Ignatius of Loyola, was converted in the isolation of disability due to battle wounds. Taken out of the action, you, too, may encounter in a more intimate way your Savior who freely sweated blood in an agony of waiting.

Prayer in uncertainty:

"O God, when will this misery end? Please shorten this time so that I can go back to normal life. I promise that when I get well I will live for your kingdom instead of wasting so much time on selfish pleasures.

"Please accept my sufferings in reparation for my sins and those of so many of my age group. Keep me from depression and despair. Give me hope in you. Thank you for all the help from my family and friends."

∼ *Scripture for Meditation* ∼

Like a swallow or a crane I clamor, I moan like a dove. My eyes are weary with looking upward. O Lord, I am oppressed; be thou my security!

ISAIAH 38:14

"Do you want to be healed?" The sick man answered him, "Sir, I have no man to put me into the pool when the water is troubled...." "Rise, take up your pallet, and walk." And at once the man was healed.

JOHN 5:6-9

With God all things are possible.

MATTHEW 19:26

I Feel As If I'm Only Half a Person Now

Is there no balm in Gilead? Is there no physician there?

JEREMIAH 8:22

"When Johnny was diagnosed with severe emphysema at the age of sixty-seven, our life together changed dramatically. It seemed as if all the fun went away. We used to do a lot of things as a couple, such as sailing, golf, and eating out. Now John sits in front of the TV with his oxygen gear. He says his life is over.

"Recently he stopped going out anywhere, even to Sunday Mass. He says he can't stand having people stare at him with the huge oxygen tank and the wheelchair. What energizes him most is reading up on lung diseases and searching out doctors with an interest in alternative treatments. When a procedure does nothing to cure or halt his worsening condition, we plunge further into discouragement.

"Lying awake in the night empathizing with his pain and defeat, I wonder what I can do to help. Being around all day seems about the only thing. He says I should go out and have fun with our old friends: 'Enjoy it double for me.' But when I kiss him goodbye, there's this mournful look in his face, so I feel guilty as if I were abandoning him.

"I try to cheer him up by getting videos of his favorite old movies and inviting the kids and grandchildren over. The little ones are OK with it, but I can tell our sons and daughters can't stand to see their strong daddy looking so weak. They make any excuse to cancel visits."

Reflection and Prayer

It's not unusual for caretakers to feel guilty about doing anything by themselves that they used to do with a chronically ill person they love. You want to show your solidarity, but you know that you can't really understand the plight of the sick person when you have never been that sick yourself. Stymied, you may seek any kind of distraction for yourself in the name of distracting the sufferer.

Trying to relax through TV or games is not wrong at all. More emphasis is needed, though, on meeting Christ together in this painful phase of your life. It could become the time of greatest closeness, a foretaste of a shared eternity.

One way of getting help with the problems of chronic illness and care taking is by joining support groups directly related to your situation. Why wouldn't Jesus, preacher of love, want you to drop your pride and confess to needing the help of veterans in your tragic situation? Leaders of such outreaches will understand the many emotional upheavals of the sick person, such as his feeling that he is only half a person now.

They will also know where you can get volunteer attendants or other services to allow for needed breaks from the strain of caretaking. You may need as well professional counseling if you find that you are not physically or emotionally able to keep up with needed care. Social workers know where to find the most skilled attendants or the best convalescent home in your area.

Before seeking out any of these helps, it is important to ask for the sacrament of the anointing of the sick from your priest. This sacrament was previously viewed as appropriate only for the dying, but for a long time now it has been administered as a healing sacrament to anyone with serious illness. This sacrament can be supplemented with daily prayer together for alleviation of pain.

If God chooses to permit the illness to continue, the sick person needs to pray for the strength to endure the humiliations that go with increasing disability. Reading Scripture and the lives of saints, many of whom suffered incredible physical pain, will help you see how to unite your sufferings with those of Jesus on the cross. This will bring spiritual benefits to yourself and those you intercede for. Many increase their hope by permeating the atmosphere of the home with beautiful religious music, large crucifixes, and pictures of the resurrection of Jesus and of the blessed.

∼ Scripture for Meditation ∼

Fear not, for I have redeemed you; I have called you by name, you are mine. When you pass through the waters I will be with you; and through the rivers, they shall not overwhelm you.... For I am the Lord your God, the Holy One of Israel, your Savior.

ISAIAH 43:1-3

And they cast out many demons, and anointed with oil many that were sick and healed them.

MARK 6:13

But as servants of God we commend ourselves in every way: through great endurance, in afflictions, hardships, calamities.

2 CORINTHIANS 6:4

Although he was a Son, he learned obedience through what he suffered; and being made perfect he became the source of eternal salvation to all who obey him.

HEBREWS 5:8-9

Don't Let Me Go Crazy!

Save me, O God! For the waters have come up to my neck. I sink in deep mire, where there is no foothold; I have come into deep waters, and the flood sweeps over me.

PSALM 69:1-2

"When my wife left me two years ago for another man, I felt as if I had died and gone to hell. Every morning I woke up, looked over at her side of the bed, turned over, and prayed God would zap me out of existence. No such luck!

"Gradually the piercing agony dissipated itself into a state of gray depression. At first I thought this was just what anyone would feel in my circumstances and would gradually disappear. Instead, it got worse!

"Six months after Pam left it reached a point where nothing and no one seemed good. I saw everyone through the dark glasses of cynicism, just waiting for each relative and friend to disillusion me. Not being able to concentrate on the newspaper or TV, I started sleeping a lot, sometimes going to bed right after dinner. Images of ending the misery through an overdose flitted through my mind in the middle of the night."

Reflection and Prayer

Professional psychological help is imperative, not only when you exhibit outwardly psychotic behavior, but also whenever you have feelings of severe depression or panic that don't go away. Only those trained in the area of mental health can distinguish clearly between symptoms that will yield to medication and those that require psychoanalysis or psychotherapy, or a combination.

For instance, some forms of depression seem to be caused by chemical imbalance, but other kinds by stress. Depression can also be a form of anger turned inward. Most doctors and psychologists insist that exercise is an important way to combat depression and anxiety as well. But Alzheimer's disease, which can seem to be an emotional problem, is now thought to be primarily physical and can be at least alleviated through appropriate medication. With all these theories out there, you may be the last person to come up with either a diagnosis or a remedy that works.

Even though God can heal you of any illness, it seems that he usually answers your prayer for help through the instrumentality of others. For example, God used the harp playing of David to heal Saul of what seems to have been severe melancholy. Where a severe negative state of mind follows upon an emotional wound caused by a person close to you, a spiritual director would certainly suggest healing through forgiveness. But if the depression persists after deep prayer for reconciliation, why not turn to mental health professionals?

Largely because of the stigma connected to nervous ailments, many Christians shun the help of professionals, who care so much that they study these matters in depth. But think about it: Though you would certainly counsel someone with a broken leg to pray, I doubt that you would tell him or her to go to the chapel *instead of* visiting the specialist!

Here is a prayer you might say as you seek help:

"Lord, I've always been a strong person. I never thought anything could get me this far down. I'm so confused. I wish you would take it away, but if you want me to seek professional help, please show me the right person to go to. Hide me in your heart during this time of estrangement from my relatives and friends. I do believe that you love me and want me to be healed."

∼ Scripture for Meditation ∼

And whenever the evil spirit ... was upon Saul, David took the lyre and played it with his hand; so Saul was refreshed, and was well, and the evil spirit departed from him.

1 SAMUEL 16:23

I am weary with my moaning; every night I flood my bed with tears.... My eye wastes away because of grief, it grows weak because of all my foes.

PSALM 6:6-7

I will solve my riddle to the music of the lyre.

PSALM 49:4

Out of the depths I cry to thee, O Lord!

PSALM 130:1

Death, Where Is Your Sting?

But God will ransom my soul from the power of Sheol, for he will receive me.

PSALM 49:15

"'I am sorry to have to tell you this, Mrs. Weigel, but your husband will probably die of this cancer within the next six months,' the doctor said on our last visit. He added: 'When the pain gets worse, you'll want to bring him to the hospital so we can help him more.'

"My husband was so weak and thin that I was expecting the bad news. Still, when the doctor actually said it, I felt as if a hammer had hit me on the head. My body went numb. When we got home I settled Ray in his recliner in the living room and took the portable phone into the kitchen to call the kids. They would want to visit him once more before the end.

"Somehow, until that announcement I still had hope. So many people were praying for him to be healed. He was only sixty. When my husband slept, I'd go into another room and cry and cry.

"It's not that I didn't believe he was going to a better place. In fact, he was suffering so much I knew he'd be better off in the hands of Jesus. Just the same, when I pictured what that horrible moment would be like when he left us, I felt this tension in my chest, as if I were going to have a heart attack."

Reflection and Prayer

In his book *Jaws of Death, Gates of Heaven*, the great Catholic philosopher Dietrich von Hildebrand explains how even for those with strong faith in eternal life, the dying of a beloved person will usually bring incredible agony. Our entire experience of this person was as an embodied soul. So trying to imagine what the separation of soul and body will be at death is almost impossible. Even many of the widow saints, in spite of great faith in life after death, suffered deeply when their husbands were dying.

Counselors of grieving groups tell us that trying to suppress sorrow in order to avoid upsetting others or for fear of breaking down only leads to problems later on. You may want to check out local hospice groups who are trained to help you and the family make this the most loving and peaceful time possible. They are also experts on the alleviation of pain.

The period when death is predicted to come soon creates special opportunities for the dying person and his or her family. Non-Catholics sometimes convert even if they have resisted such a move up until this time. Reconciliations that seemed impossible to bring about often take place when time is running out. If you know of any loose ends concerning forgiveness issues, now would be a good time to try to bring the people involved to peace, if only on the phone for those who live far away.

At hospitals, Catholic chaplains call the priest to come and offer general confession. If you know or suspect that your beloved one has grave sins on his or her conscience, it is necessary that they receive absolution. Receiving the anointing of the sick may not bring remission of the illness, but it always brings special interior healing graces.

If the dying person is at home, you should be sure to call the priest.

Members of the family as well as friends should be given private time with the dying person for last words.

Even if your loved one has not been devout up to this point, you may find that in this crisis the desire for Holy Communion, meditation on Scripture, and prayer will greatly increase. God will have special graces for you as well, even if you are too distraught to sense them in the present. "One day at a time" is a fine phrase to repeat to yourself as you try to show the most love during this crisis. Talking about death as "going home" can be comforting to all of you.

The words of the rosary have a poignancy at this time. All those who gather at the beside of the dying person may want to join you as you pray:

"Hail Mary, full of grace, the Lord is with you. Blessed are you among women, and blessed is the fruit of your womb, Jesus. Holy Mary, Mother of God, pray for us sinners now and at the hour of our death. Amen."

∼ Scripture for Meditation ∼

Let me dwell in thy tent for ever! Oh to be safe under the shelter of thy wings!

PSALM 61:4

My dwelling is plucked up and removed from me like a shepherd's tent; like a weaver I have rolled up my life; he cuts me off from the loom; from day to night thou dost bring me to an end; I cry for help until morning; like a lion he breaks all my bones; from day to night thou dost bring me to an end.

ISAIAH 38:12-13

The Lord will save me, and we will sing to stringed instruments all the days of our life, at the house of the Lord.

ISAIAH 38:20

"Your brother will rise again." Martha said to him, "I know that he will rise again in the resurrection at the last day." Jesus said to her, "I am the resurrection and the life; he who believes in me, though he die, yet shall he live, and whoever lives and believes in me shall never die. Do you believe this?"

JOHN 11:23-26

At the Gates of Eternity

But our commonwealth is in heaven, and from it we await a
Savior, the Lord Jesus Christ, who will change our lowly body to
be like his glorious body, by the power which enables him even
to subject all things to himself.

PHILIPPIANS 3:20-21

"Part of me wants to die. Ever since I found Christ in the Church in a new way during my adult conversion, I wanted to be with him fully, face-to-face, for all eternity. I long to kiss his feet. I long to embrace those I loved personally and those I admired so much, such as the saints, and never be separated from them again.

"But there is another part of me that is in 'fear and trembling.' What will my all-holy Jesus say about my sins? What will he say about all those times when there was something good I could do, but I preferred instead what was easier?

"The faces of those who have despised or ridiculed me arise before me during the long nights of my dying. Suppose they are right? Suppose those are right who think life is only 'a tale told by an idiot, signifying nothing,' as Shakespeare described how skeptics see it? Suppose the pain of my last moments is so terrible that I go insane and my last words are crazed blasphemies?"

Reflection and Prayer

In the next chapter we will offer wisdom and comfort for the bereaved. Here will be inspiration for the dying person.

The Danish theologian Søren Kierkegaard once said that the approach of death has an eloquence that surpasses the words of any preacher! Sensing imminent death, you are forced to make a final leap of faith into the arms of the God of merciful love. As you prepare for this change in your state of being, you will need to focus not only on the meaning of your own life, but on the purpose of life itself.

You will probably notice that your thoughts change depending on whether you are brooding within yourself or immersing yourself in God. Thoughts of God, the unchanging Absolute, or thoughts of the sublime beauty you have found in nature and in those you have loved most profoundly cause the fear and shame to abate. This is because your eternal soul is akin to goodness and beauty. Your experiences of them have been given by God to give you hope. They are a foretaste of heaven.

If doubt comes, tempting you to despair that you are nothing but a piece of dying matter, you need to consider that your unique personhood, the one that has been you from conception, cannot possibly be material. The proof that your soul is a spiritual reality is that it cannot be measured or weighed as all material things can. So when the material body dies, it cannot take your soul with it into the grave.

Be consoled by the truth that everything you are leaving was created by God. There is no beauty or lovableness in them that is not a reflection of the same qualities in perfect, absolute form in God. And in the new heaven and new earth, you will enter at once, or after purgatorial purification, you will find all you have loved in transfigured glory.

The saints seem to have been given superior insights into life with the God for whom they sacrificed so much. St. Francis welcomed the end of life on earth by calling it Sister Death. Revived after an apparent death, St. Teresa of Avila, a woman Doctor of the Church, was asked what death was like. She proclaimed: "Death is ecstasy!"

Of inspiration and comfort when you are at the gates of eternity are the readings to be found in the Liturgy of the Hours' Office of the Dead. If you don't have that book, you might open your Bible and meditate on the Psalms included in the Office of the Dead: Psalms 40, 42, 51, 70, 85, 86, 121, 130, 146, 150. Inserting your name or that of the one you love as you read can make it even more personal, as in "Ronda, like a deer that yearns for running streams..." Repeating the words of the Our Father and Hail Mary, acts of contrition, and favorite litanies can also bring peace.

What prayer could be better for you in your last hours than the one Jesus said on the cross? "Into your hands I commend my spirit."

~ Scripture for Meditation ~

I know that my Redeemer lives and,... after my skin has been thus destroyed, then [from] my flesh I shall see God.

JOB 19:25-26

In Christ shall all be made alive. But each in his own order: Christ the first fruits, then at his coming those who belong to Christ.

1 CORINTHIANS 15:22-23

For this perishable nature must put on the imperishable, and this mortal nature must put on immortality.... "Death is swallowed up in victory."

1 CORINTHIANS 15:53-54

[Christ] became obedient unto death, even death on a cross.

PHILIPPIANS 2:8

Five

Wipe Away Our Tears!

When Jesus saw [Martha] weeping, and the Jews who came with her also weeping, he was deeply moved in spirit and troubled.

JOHN 11:33

Even if a beloved person who dies is a canonizable saint who you believe is going straight to heaven, you most likely will feel overwhelmed by the loss. This is especially true when the person who died is someone you have depended on. Death is probably easiest to accept when the relationship was good, the deceased lived far away, and he or she was looking forward to death as release from pain or a long-awaited union with God.

Those in grief ministry claim that when you lose someone who was a basic part of your life, such as a parent, close sibling, child, or best friend, grieving is necessary. Keeping a stiff upper lip, fighting back the tears, going about your business as if nothing happened, is supposed to be the worst course to take, at least for most of us. If you don't allow yourself to feel the pain, it will usually emerge in some other way, such as depression, anxiety, despair, or doubt.

Most bereaved people feel numb at first. Still they need to talk to someone about their feelings. Going to a parish or neighborhood grief group can be more beneficial than you can imagine.

When you are overwhelmed, it is also good to exercise or engage in physical projects such as house cleaning or yard work. Being immersed in the beauty of nature or music can remind you that there is something besides anguish on this earth, something to help you believe in eternity. It is especially helpful to read Scripture texts such as those you will see quoted in this chapter to keep bolstering your faith in the world to come, where you hope to be reunited with your beloved dead.

If you begin to feel you can't go on, you need to see a professional therapist.

The narratives, reflections, and prayers to follow will touch on specific feelings coming from the loss of parents, spouses, children, and other people whose death can be overwhelming. If the type of relationship in which you have experienced a loss is not mentioned here, ask the Holy Spirit to comfort you in a personal way.

I'm an Orphan!

"When my mother called me to say Dad was killed in a multiple car wreck, I couldn't believe it. My whole body went numb. 'I'll be on the next plane,' I finally muttered.

" 'Take care; don't drive too fast going to the airport,' my Mom said through her tears.

"On the plane, the selfish thought flitted through my mind that I might have to drop out of college unless he had lots of life insurance. Basically, I knew that nothing would be the same after this tragedy. Since I'm the oldest son, I prayed that God would make me strong for Mom and the younger kids.

" 'My God!' I prayed. 'Jimmy's only five. He's hardly going to remember what Dad was like when he grows up! We're all orphans now!'

"At the funeral Mass I couldn't concentrate on the words the priest was saying. Instead I kept thinking: *God, why did you have to let this happen? Dad was the best man I've ever known. He prayed every day, went to Mass on Sunday even on vacation, tithed to the Church, and gave to the poor.*

"That first week I was too busy helping out even to try to get an answer to those questions. Back at college, though, I started skipping Sunday Mass."

Reflection and Prayer

Sometimes our parents outlive us, but usually they die before we do. Becoming an orphan is always difficult, but the impact of the experience varies according to a person's age. Psychologists tell us that when the orphan is young, it is necessary for a surviving parent or relatives to help the child deal with the loss rather than be silent about it.

Emphasis needs to be placed on defusing the belief many youngsters have that they are somehow to blame for the death. This idea is common because when punished, a child will sometimes unconsciously wish the parent were dead.

Telling a young child that God took the parent is not always such a good idea. If God suddenly decides to take people, the child may reason, then everyone else around may disappear soon as well. It would be better to say something like this: "Probably all of us will live long lives, and one day you'll see your dad [mom] in heaven."

If you describe what heaven will be like, you will give the orphan child some kind of image to hold onto. It is also important to try to find in the family or among friends an older person who can fulfill some of the roles played by the missing parent.

If you are a teen who has lost a parent, your grief may be complicated by other feelings. You may need to accept the fact, without guilt, that if your dead parent was controlling or unsympathetic to your needs, you may have a sense of liberation. This can also be the case with the death of a sibling who was an occasion for rivalry or jealousy.

On the other hand, if the relationship was good, you may feel cheated. *My parent will be missing,* you suddenly realize, *when I graduate, on my wedding day, when I get my first good job, when my children are born, when I take my vows or get ordained.* If the parent's death means a loss of income and many consequent sacrifices on your part, these consequences may be resented. Anger at God for permitting all this to happen is not uncommon.

An exercise that has helped many young or old after the loss of a parent, especially if the death was sudden, is to write him or her a "letter." In this letter you pour out feelings such as these: "Dear Dad, I miss you so much. I feel awful that we never got to say good-bye. Did you know how much I loved you?" Or, if there was conflict: "Dear Mom, I never got to forgive you or to ask you to forgive me. I promise to pray for your soul. Please pray for me." It is good to include specifics.

Next, you can ask the Holy Spirit to help you compose the letter in reply that your parent would write if he or she had access to a pen. You may be surprised how real that letter can be.

A prayer after the loss of a parent:

"I do believe that my dad [mom] is in your hands, dear Jesus. You know all the turmoil I am going through. Help me to endure the pain. Help me to trust in your promise of eternal life. Please shorten my parent's time in purgatory. As I go on with my life, help me believe in the invisible loving presence of my parent. Please send me other men or women to father or mother me as I need."

~ *Scripture for Meditation* ~

[The Lord's] kindness has not forsaken the living or the dead!

RUTH 2:20

He will swallow up death for ever, and the Lord God will wipe away tears from all faces.

ISAIAH 25:8

And I heard a voice from heaven saying,... "Blessed are the dead who die in the Lord ... that they may rest from their labors, for their deeds follow them!"

REVELATION 14:13

Why Did My Child Have to Die So Young?

A voice was heard in Ramah, wailing and loud lamentation, Rachel weeping for her children; she refused to be consoled, because they were no more.

MATTHEW 2:18

"'Sudden death syndrome.' They even nickname it 'SDS!' Our dear little firstborn Marie, only three months old. It was a year ago, and we still cry ourselves to sleep. I finally closed the door to her little room and gave the crib to the Salvation Army so I wouldn't have to see it anymore.

"Our friends say she's our family angel in heaven interceding for us. That's a lovely image, but it doesn't take away the grief. At the funeral the priest said that in spite of our sorrow we should realize that this child will never sin.

"Our greatest wish for her was that one day she would go to heaven and live in eternal bliss. We trust that this prayer has been answered, yes. But if we live a normal span, how many years till we get to see her face-to-face again?

"I'm pregnant again, but full of fear. And I'm afraid that my fear will somehow seep into the body of this baby and weaken it. Of course, we've read up on SDS, and this time we'll be prepared with everything modern medicine has devised for early detection and pre-vention. But I doubt if we'll be able to breathe easy until our second child lives past the first year."

Reflection and Prayer

The death of a wee one brings a sadness of its own kind. Since you know that death came into the world with the fall of our first parents, you are less willing to accept it when it comes to the innocent than when it comes to adult sinners. The helplessness of tiny babies evokes protective parental instincts to the maximum. That you weren't able to save your baby can add a false sense of guilt to your helplessness.

With miscarriage, the parents often do not get to see the baby. Hospital nurses are instructed to break the sac and immerse the baby in water, saying the words of baptism over him or her. It is a help in the grieving process to name the child and conduct some kind of prayer service. Some cemeteries have special memorial plaques for the miscarried and for grieved aborted babies.

Remember that this tiny child will always be a member of the family, and you can one day meet in eternity. Grief ministers recommend that parents and siblings hold a stillborn baptized child in their arms, talking to him or her and praying before burial.

The death of an older child still in youth, through illness, accident, or other tragedy, can be even more painful because of the number of years you have known and loved him or her. There is a feeling of consternation. You think you should die first, since this is more common, at least, in countries with modern medicine available.

Constant churning over the possibility that the death could have been prevented is for some inevitable. There is no point in trying to force yourself to accept it when you aren't yet able to. It is usually a long, long time before you can resign yourself to the fact that God allowed it to happen for his own reasons.

When you obtain the grace truly to believe that your child is better off with Jesus than on earth, you will be able to release the hold your grief has on him or her. Pray for that knowledge.

Spending time with other parents who have lost a child, especially parents with strong faith, will ease the pain somewhat. Support groups led by trained people will help you see how common are feelings such as anger, no matter how unexpected. Parents whose children have died say it is important not to fixate on the time of death, but to spend time in the family recalling happy times.

Burying feelings of hurt or fear is never good. Including the beloved child in your daily prayers brings a sense of solidarity.

When the child who dies is an adult of any age, things are more complicated. Most importantly, you should never picture your child as a body alone in the grave. The God who created this unique person is surely able to sustain his or her soul in his divine heart. Always picture your child wrapped in the arms of Jesus.

A prayer for a child who died:

"May the souls of the faithful departed rest in peace. Lord of life, I give you and Mother Mary my beloved child to have and to hold. Keep me from doubt and despair. I beg you to give me the trust to believe in the reality of the unseen world where there are no more tears."

～ Scripture for Meditation ～

"It is my son's robe; a wild beast has devoured him...." Then Jacob rent his garments, and put sackcloth upon his loins, and mourned for his son many days.... He refused to be comforted, and said, "No, I shall go down to Sheol to my son, mourning."

GENESIS 37:33-35

Would I had died instead of you, O Absalom, my son, my son!

2 SAMUEL 18:33

The Lord gave, and the Lord has taken away; blessed be the name of the Lord.

JOB 1:21

And all were weeping and bewailing her; but [Jesus] said, "Do not weep; for she is not dead but sleeping.... Child, arise." And her spirit returned, and she got up at once.

LUKE 8:52-55

"Till Death Do Us Part"

Be still, and know that I am God.

PSALM 46:10

"My wife, Liz, died five months ago of Alzheimer's. The last years of our marriage were incredibly sad as more and more of her reason went. One of our daughters, a nurse, took a leave of absence from her paying job and stayed with us for the last terrible year. In spite of how much I prayed that God would take her, when it finally happened I was devastated.

"I walk around the house that is full of ghosts of the past with my heart like a dead weight in my body. My adult children and grandkids visit as often as possible, but who can replace my wife of forty-five years? Every time they come, my children urge me to sell the house and move in with one of them. They don't seem to understand.

"The house is what I have left of Liz. My wife was a real homebody. Every room is full of the things she treasured: photos of the children and grandchildren at all ages, the books she read to each of them, old toys kept for the grandchildren to play with when they visited, the dishes we ate on. Our whole life is in this house.

"In the evening I sit on the back porch. When I close my eyes and pray to God, sometimes I feel her presence next to me. I can almost hear her whisper: 'Don't cry, honey. Not too long, and we'll be together again.'

"Then I understand better that line from the Psalms, 'Be still, and know that I am God.' Since I myself am not God, I can't bring her back or predict how long till I die. But God knows everything. He is in charge ... and it's going to be all right. When I go to Mass now, the words about the next life really stand out."

Reflection and Prayer

Life is a pilgrimage. Our home is not here on earth but in heaven. When the person with whom you were "two in one flesh" dies, it feels as if half of you is gone to the next world. Sometimes the image that comes to mind is that your tears of grief are like a river to sail into the heart of God.

When a marriage has been good, there is sweetness mingled with sadness. When a marriage has been difficult, there are surprises. No longer seeing yourself as the victim of the other's flaws, it is clearer what the virtues were that you now miss so much.

The death of a spouse usually involves decisions about change. There are some exceptions: Queen Victoria insisted on maintaining a table setting for her beloved spouse, Prince Albert, after his death and kept his clothing as if in readiness for his return! Other bereaved husbands and wives, however, feel a need to give everything away so as not to be haunted by memories.

The opinions of others, even close family, about such decisions can be irritating. Better to ask the Holy Spirit what to do day by day as your way of mourning and your way of opening to new life. Did you know that quite a number of widows are becoming consecrated women, and some widowers are becoming priests?

As a Catholic believer you can take comfort in having Masses said for your beloved spouse and also praying often at home for his or her soul on that unseen pilgrimage toward eternity. Most dioceses have "new beginnings" groups for widows and widowers. At times of the most piercing sorrow, identify with Jesus on the cross, perhaps making the Stations.

Ask Mary to help you. She grieved for St. Joseph. This is a time when God wants to be close, a time of spiritual deepening. The person you probably took for granted much of your life has entered into the mystery of mysteries. What is she or he telling you about the meaning of your life?

A prayer when you have lost your spouse:

"O my God, I had no idea how awful I would feel. Thank you so much for everything wonderful about my beloved. I feel sorry for those times when we didn't get along well.

"When I go to sacramental confession next, help me remember my sins against my wife or husband so that my contrition may somehow be freeing and healing to the soul that is most probably now in purgatory. Show me what you want me to do with my loneliness. Whether you want me to move closer to the children to be a comfort and helper to them, or to start out on a completely new lifestyle, please show me!"

~ *Scripture for Meditation* ~

Thou dost show me the path of life; in thy presence there is fulness of joy, in thy right hand are pleasures for evermore.

PSALM 16:11

It is full time now for you to wake from sleep. For salvation is nearer to us now than when we first believed.

ROMANS 13:11

Through him you have confidence in God, who raised him from the dead and gave him glory, so that your faith and hope are in God.

1 PETER 1:21

My Leaning Post Has Relocated!

He who conquers shall be clad thus in white garments, and I will not blot his name out of the book of life; I will confess his name before my Father and before his angels.

REVELATION 3:5

"I went through a terrible time when my husband abandoned me and the children four years ago to marry another woman. It was such a shock. It seems he dated this woman on sales trips in another state.

"A friend of mine in the parish suggested that I go to the charismatic prayer group. She was sure I needed extra grace to get through this change. The priest who led the group was Fr. Meyers, a fatherly priest in his fifties.

"The loud praise and the prophecies were a welcome distraction from brooding about my family problems. At one of the healing Masses Fr. Meyers called out that there was a woman whose husband had left her who was suffering from low self-esteem. I went up at the end of the service to be prayed over.

"When he prayed over me I felt the first sense of healing since my husband left. Afterwards I went to him for spiritual counseling. He got me going to daily Mass and taught me to read Scripture before bed instead of watching sitcoms.

"After awhile it got to where the high point of my week was meeting this priest for direction before the prayer meeting. I'd never met such a wonderful, understanding, holy priest. When he died suddenly of cardiac arrest in the middle of Mass one evening, it felt like the end of the world for me.

"A friend in the prayer group suggested another priest I could go to for confession and direction, but I didn't want to dig up my whole story again for a stranger. I still go to Mass every day, but it feels dry and perfunctory. Why couldn't God have let such a fine priest live longer?"

Prayer and Reflection

God can work in a powerful way to bring you closer to him through the mediation of holy men and women. Abstract ideas of sanctity become real for you when you see them embodied in a person you know. After a few years of being discipled by such a leader, you have taken in many of his or her ideas, and in some ways you represent those truths in your own person.

If the love of the holy friend comes at a time when you are broken by life's tragedies, sometimes the bond has a psychological aspect as well. This aspect can be healing unless it goes to extremes. *Codependence* is a term devised by some experts on human behavior to describe relationships in which the bond becomes too tight. A spiritual leader is meant to be a bridge to Jesus—the only perfect friend. He or she is not meant to be a pseudo-spouse or parent.

It is natural and good to grieve the death of someone who has brought you closer to God. But remember that after death your friend will still be united to you in a supernatural manner. There is no way such a person can be simply replaced because of your need. Still, in the last analysis, a holy man or woman is an image of the beauty of Jesus.

When he or she dies, this is a time to let go and place both your hands into those of Jesus. He wants you for himself for awhile. Later he will send you other friends on your journey to final union with him.

This poem of St. Teresa of Avila is worth learning by heart to pray whenever feelings of desperation about the loss of a beloved mentor won't give way to reason:

Let nothing disturb thee,
Nothing affright thee;
All things are passing;
God never changeth;
Patient endurance
Attaineth to all things;
Who God possesseth
In nothing is wanting;
Alone God sufficeth.

When your feeling of loss becomes acute, these are some words you could pray:

"Thank you, Lord, for the great gift of a holy mentor at a time of emotional crisis for me. I don't know what would have become of me without this person's loving care. I do believe that he or she is presently praising you in heaven in glory.

"Please let a particle of this light into my troubled heart. Don't let me insult you by acting as if you can't give me directly what you gave me through my friend. I surrender myself to you, body, soul, mind, and heart. Take me to yourself and give me peace."

∼ Scripture for Meditation ∼

Love is strong as death.

SONG OF SOLOMON 8:6

After two days he will revive us; on the third day he will raise us up, that we may live before him.... Let us press on to know the Lord; his going forth is sure as the dawn.

HOSEA 6:2-3

You did not choose me, but I chose you and appointed you that you should go and bear fruit and that your fruit should abide.

JOHN 15:16

The Enigma of Suicide

For thou dost not give me up to Sheol.

PSALM 16:10

"Why? Why? Why? My son had everything going for him. He was a fine student. Everyone loved him for his joy, loving heart, and wonderful sense of humor.

"They say suicide is an enigma. No matter what problems the suicide faced, there are millions of others with the same or worse who live on in hope. For me, the enigma is how I survived the unbearable news that my son died of an overdose.

"In the note he left, my twenty-year-old boy said that the agony of living was too much for him. He prayed God would forgive him. He hoped we could forgive him.

"In hindsight, it was clear he was going through severe manic-depression at the time of his dread deed. Even though his friends tried to warn us, we didn't realize how close he was to taking his life. This was because he concealed the negative side under the mask of a clown.

"I can't stop wondering whether he would have been saved had we forced him into an institution for mandatory therapy and medication. Now I tell everyone I meet who knows a despairing person not to trust their own intuitions but to rush the potential suicide to professional help."

Reflection and Prayer

The thought that a loved one freely chose to leave us makes suicide especially painful. There are grieving groups called Survivors of Suicide for those left behind. If someone close to you committed suicide, you might benefit from one of these groups, which are free of charge.

There has been a development in Christian teaching concerning the supernatural destiny of someone who took his or her own life. Formerly, people thought that suicides could never be forgiven. Hell would then be the only place for one whose last act was a mortal sin. Yet due to a greater understanding of psychology, without denying the sin, there has come a greater understanding of factors limiting responsibility.

If you were close to a person who died by his or her own will, you need to ponder carefully these words of hope from the *Catechism of the Catholic Church* (2280-83): "We are stewards, not owners, of the life God has entrusted to us. It is not ours to dispose of.... Grave psychological disturbances, anguish, or grave fear of hardship, suffering, or torture can diminish the responsibility of the one committing suicide. We should not despair of the eternal salvation of persons who have taken their own lives. By ways known to him alone, God can provide the opportunity for salutary repentance. The Church prays for persons who have taken their own lives."

Instead of despairing, you need to fling your hopes for the soul of the suicide into the ocean of Jesus' mercy. Only he can save this tortured soul, who may have repented minutes before death. Only trust in our Lord can assuage your agony.

A prayer for a suicide:

"'Lord have mercy! Christ have mercy! Lord have mercy!' 'For the sake of your sorrowful passion, have mercy on us and on the whole world.'

"I beg you to save the dear one who in desperation took his or her own life. I believe that you love this person a thousand times more than I do. I believe that at the last moment you offered him or her your divine embrace.

"Please accept my prayers and sufferings now to join to your redemption of this soul. According to your wisdom, I beg you for a sign that my beloved one is saved."

∼ Scripture for Meditation ∼

Thou hast held back my life from the pit of destruction, for thou has cast all my sins behind thy back.

ISAIAH 38:17

Therefore [Judas Maccabeus] made atonement for the dead, that they might be delivered from their sin.

2 MACCABEES 12:45

But God shows his love for us in that while we were yet sinners Christ died for us. Since, therefore, we are now justified by his blood, much more shall we be saved by him from the wrath of God.

ROMANS 5:8-9

Six

Lord, I Believe; Help My Unbelief!

Now Thomas, one of the twelve ... was not with them when Jesus came.... "Unless I see in his hands the print of the nails, and place my finger in the mark of the nails, and place my hand in his side, I will not believe."

JOHN 20:24-25

Even those brought up as strong Christians sometimes go through periods of doubt. The state of doubt is not a purely intellectual matter, since it can lead into despair, laxity, and sometimes sin. Only the God of love can give us the courage to live right. For this reason, entering into a crisis of faith can be overwhelming.

If nothing is sacred, why sacrifice for anything? As the Russian Christian novelist Fyodor Dostoevsky put it, for those for whom God is dead, no crime is unjustifiable. Those who doubt God's reality can come, at least for a time, to rationalizing sin as liberation.

No matter how frightening doubt may become, we need to know that it can also be a step toward stronger faith. The most seemingly innocent and unsophisticated saints such as Thérèse of Lisieux, the Little Flower, experienced times when the light of faith was all but extinguished as they battled with dark doubts. But with God's grace the saints emerged with faith as gold purified by fire.

In this chapter we will come to grips with doubts of God's existence, doubts of his love, doubts that religious practice is meaningful, doubts about the Catholic Church as the only fully true way. If you are an ardent believer who has not significantly doubted your faith, pray for all those represented by the narratives in this section.

I'm Not Sure There Is a God

The fool says in his heart, "There is no God."

PSALM 14:1

"I come from a totally Catholic family. I mean my parents go to daily Mass, prayer meetings, and every Catholic conference within three hundred miles! When I was home, I just went along. My doubts began in college. I chose to go out of town to a state university because I wanted to be a nurse, a major not offered in the Catholic colleges near us.

"At first I went to Mass every Sunday and hung out with other Christians. I stayed away from the party students. In my sophomore year I took an elective in philosophy. I was surprised that the professor took it for granted that there was no God and that religion was some kind of scam preying on the ignorant. Actually, Dr. Blake was a Marxist.

"I figured I would have no trouble arguing against such a stupid position. Wrong! First she taught us the basics of theory of knowledge. Most of us became skeptics. I mean, really, how can anyone pretend to be sure about such huge things as the meaning of life?

"Then she took us through the most popular arguments for the existence of God. She got us to see that these so-called proofs couldn't stand up to modern reasoning. It was sad to think that my family could be so wrong. I'm not going to challenge them. I guess they need the comfort of thinking there's a God of love up there taking care of them.

"Actually, I'm confused. Most of the time I think my philosophy professor was right. Then I see a film about someone like Mother Teresa of Calcutta, and I think there's got to be a God to inspire anyone to sacrifice the way she did."

Reflection and Prayer

In his encyclical *Fides et Ratio,* John Paul II says that to be able to soar in your Catholic belief, you need two wings: faith and reason. Before Vatican II, the way faith was taught to young people included a large infusion of philosophy. Reasons for your beliefs were adapted to different age levels. Hardly anyone studying the old catechism or going to Catholic schools would ever have thought that faith was a matter of personal preference based only on individual experience.

Nowadays, even in families where there is a strong commitment to the faith, the intellectual side of Catholic heritage is not often emphasized. When you run into the arguments against the faith by scholarly opponents, you may find yourself overwhelmed by doubt.

One of the quickest ways to bolster your knowledge about God's existence and nature is to read the section in the *Catechism of the Catholic Church* entitled "Man's Capacity for God" (27-49). Briefly stated, the *Catechism* says this: The world we see around us, including the skeptics in it, could not exist at all unless there was an absolute, unchanging eternal cause outside the world.

Everything around us changes. There was no necessity for anything material ever to exist. Given an infinite amount of time, there would have to be one time when nothing existed. If there was ever nothing, how could anything come forth from it? Only if the foundation of the universe is an all-powerful Being that cannot *not* exist could anything else come forth. (See the resource list at the end of this book for where to find proofs for God's existence, including those advanced by contemporary scientists.)

When you have read more on this topic, you will appreciate the amusing challenge of the Danish philosopher Søren Kierkegaard. He recalled that it was a shock when Copernicus convinced scientists that our planet was not the center of the universe, with the sun circling us, but rather that we were circling with the other planets around the sun. Kierkegaard remarked that by analogy, there is a Copernican revolution in the soul of a man when he realizes it is not he who is the center of the universe, judging God, but rather it is God who is at the center, judging him.

While you are seeking the truth, you might try the famous skeptic's prayer: "God, if there is a God, save my soul, if I have a soul." Less humorously: "God, please show me that you exist in a way that will be convincing to me personally."

~ *Scripture for Meditation* ~

Teach me wisdom in my secret heart.

PSALM 51:6

A man's wisdom makes his face shine, and the hardness of his countenance is changed.

ECCLESIASTES 8:1

For what can be known about God is plain to [the ungodly], because God has shown it to them. Ever since the creation of the world his invisible nature, namely, his eternal power and deity, has been clearly perceived in the things that have been made.... But they became futile in their thinking and their senseless minds were darkened.

ROMANS 1:19-21

Why Get Close to a God Who Permits So Much Evil?

The Lord answered Job out of the whirlwind:... "Will you even put me in the wrong? Will you condemn me that you may be justified?"

JOB 40:6-8

"From boyhood I always hated injustice, like when kids tormented other kids. I'd also question my mother about why God permitted injustice. Couldn't he have stopped Cain from murdering Abel? How could God stand by while thousands of hard-working poor people starved during famines? Why wouldn't he send the rain to end a drought? And how about all those babies destroyed by abortion?

"My Catholic high school teacher tried to explain. God allows sin because he loves free will. He bails out the victims with supernatural rewards. He could have made robots, but he chose to make humans with the awesome power to choose good. What about sufferings that don't come from sin but from natural causes such as droughts? God allows these, she said, to help us realize that the earth is not our true home.

"These kinds of answers made sense until it hit where it hurt the most: myself. My fall involved profiting from a shoddy business practice. There was a product that looked good but would break down quickly. For this reason we got it cheap from the manufacturer but could sell it for a big markup.

"I was tempted because I could get enough commissions on the profits to put a down payment on a house, the first one for my little family. After a short struggle, I went along with the other salespeople. I compromised my integrity out of greed, and we made a fortune on those sales.

"Sitting around in my beautiful new home, I couldn't put it out of my head. Sure I shouldn't have done it, but what kind of God puts us into such dilemmas? I'm sure there is a God. How could so incredible a thing as our world exist by chance?

"Still, I wonder what this God is really like. Sometimes he seems more like a torturer than a God of love. When I watch clips of disasters on TV news, I mutter: 'So what were you doing when *that* happened, God of love?'"

Reflection and Prayer

Some believers try to get around the doubts described above by giving up the idea that God is perfect. They decide instead that he is great, but not able to control all the bad stuff. He needs our help. The comic filmmaker Woody Allen likes to quip about this view: "God isn't evil, he's just an underachiever!"

Of course, this is a ridiculous solution. God by his very nature is perfect.

One of the best books to read on the subject of why a God of love allows suffering is *The Problem of Pain* by C.S. Lewis. His argument is that we want to think that a loving God would arrange things for our maximum pleasure on earth. But God wants something better for us than our own way.

The real God prefers a world of free will persons and the ensuing drama of our choices, redemption, salvation. There will be joy on earth and much more so in heaven, but it is of a kind infinitely better than we would get from simply having our way.

A piercing truth about God's mysterious ways comes from Corrie ten Boom, the saintly Dutch woman who was imprisoned in a concentration camp by the Nazis for hiding Jews. In the film about her experience, *The Hiding Place*, we hear this answer to the challenge of others in the camp about how God could let all the horror happen: "If you know Jesus," she said, "you don't have to know why."

Reading books about those who have suffered unimaginable tragedy but come out with their faith strengthened, such as Viktor Frankl's *Man's Search for Meaning,* will help liberate you from the quicksand of chronic doubts into new perspectives.

You also need to get rid of an image you might have that God sits complacently in heaven counting up our merits or demerits as we suffer humbly or rebelliously. Since Jesus is the heart of the Father made more visibly known, remember his attitude toward those who suffered. You need to realize that God is present with you and those you care about as you or they suffer. He is empathizing, commiserating, holding your hands, urging to repentance, and trying to bring good out of the evil that is happening, whether caused by others, nature, or even you. The crucified Jesus is our final proof that God is not an indifferent tyrant.

In these or your own words, you might pray when doubt overwhelms you:

"Thank you, God, for all the goodness, beauty, and love in my world. I know that the pain in the world is not a matter of 'I, the perfect one, vs. them, the evil ones.' Help me to get closer to your Son so that I may truly believe that he is the answer. Send your Holy Spirit to bring me to surrender so that like Job I may be reconciled with new trust and hope."

∼ Scripture for Meditation ∼

You love righteousness and hate wickedness.

PSALM 45:7

In a time of favor I have answered you, in a day of salvation I have helped you.

ISAIAH 49:8

We have this treasure in earthen vessels, to show that the transcendent power belongs to God and not to us. We are afflicted in every way, but not crushed; perplexed, but not driven to despair.

2 CORINTHIANS 4:7-8

If any of you lacks wisdom, let him ask God.... But let him ask in faith, with no doubting, for he who doubts is like a wave of the sea that is driven and tossed by the wind.

JAMES 1:5-6

I Go to Church, But My Faith Is Weak

The word is near you, on your lips and in your heart (that is, the word of faith which we preach); because if you confess with your lips that Jesus is Lord and believe in your heart that God raised him from the dead, you will be saved.

ROMANS 10:8-9

"My parents were conservative Catholics. I was brought up to believe whatever the Church teaches. I never questioned anything until I went to a Catholic college where most of the professors were liberals.

"At first I was startled when even priests said that missing Sunday Mass was not a mortal sin. But it made sense. The main thing is to be close to God and be a loving person, not to follow a bunch of rules slavishly. My ethics professor explained that being a contemporary Catholic doesn't mean throwing out everything. It means studying the tradition and what modern theologians say, and then bringing it to prayer and making up your own mind.

"This seemed good at first, but when I was faced with hard decisions such as premarital sex, and now contraception as a married woman, I found it wasn't so easy to sort it all out. The two priests at our parish disagree about most things. This makes it even harder, because the liberal one has a warmer personality. So I prefer to go to him for counsel, but the conservative one seems more logical.

"I still go to Church most Sundays and confession once or twice a year, but it feels more like a duty than a joy. When I go up to receive the bread and wine, I think, 'Who knows whether this is the Body and Blood or just a symbol?'"

Reflection and Prayer

Polarizing parishioners or academics as conservative vs. liberal is a mistake. It can create the illusion that everything is a matter of style or general point of view rather than a matter of truth. Since you repeat at least once a week in the Nicene Creed that you believe in "one, holy, Catholic, and apostolic Church," the only position that follows is orthodox belief in matters of faith and morals.

True teaching is a precious gift of the Lord to his Church to help us find our way. For instance, the Church insists that, except in cases of illness or difficulty in finding a Mass due to distance or travel, we are obliged to go to Church every Sunday. What could be more important on the Sabbath, the day devoted to the Lord, than hearing his Word and receiving his Body and Blood in Communion?

What is legitimately open to question is prudential wisdom. Principles are unchanging, but applications can be controversial. Catholics can legitimately disagree, for example, about whether a political initiative will be effective, or whether to receive with reverence Communion in the hand or on the tongue.

Because of the ferment after Vatican II, there is a crisis in faith that includes even some bishops. Listening to preaching, reading articles in Catholic papers and magazines, and especially reading the secular press on religious issues will sometimes only cloud things more. One sure way to find out the reasons for what the Church teaches is to read the official *Catechism of the Catholic Church* coming from the Vatican, as well as other official documents.

Many Catholics in the average parish have only the foggiest notion of what is really taught by the Church on some topics. As a practicing Catholic you have an obligation to clear up doubt through prayerful study of these truths. It will be a joy for you to see how clear, logical, and life-giving are beliefs you may once have thought were shaky.

The *Catechism* is full of references to the writings of the Fathers and Doctors of the Church and quotations from the saints. Nothing could be better for further reading than study of these great writers. If you don't have the time or background to pursue such reading, watch talks on Catholic TV channels such as EWTN or read Catholic literature clearly in conformity with the Magisterium. This can be an easy way to let the splendor of truth infuse your doubtful mind.

A prayer for the weak in faith:

"God, you know that even though I am weak, I have a sincere desire to know your truth and follow it. Please forgive me for anything I have done that was not your will. In the case of serious matters, I promise that when my mind is clearer I will go to sacramental confession about sins I could have known better than to commit. May the Holy Spirit remind me to read and study the books that can help me follow you—the way, the truth, and the life."

∼ Scripture for Meditation ∼

Fight the good fight of the faith; take hold of the eternal life to which you were called.

1 Timothy 6:12

I know whom I have believed, and I am sure that he is able to guard until that Day what has been entrusted to me. Follow the pattern of the sound words which you have heard from me, in the faith and love which are in Christ Jesus; guard the truth that has been entrusted to you.

2 TIMOTHY 1:12-14

I know your works: you are neither cold nor hot. Would that you were cold or hot! So, because you are lukewarm, and neither cold nor hot, I will spew you out of my mouth.

REVELATION 3:15-16

I Don't Believe There's Only One Path

For he has made known to us in all wisdom and insight the mystery of his will, according to his purpose which he set forth in Christ as a plan for the fulness of time, to unite all things in him, things in heaven and things on earth.

EPHESIANS 1:9-10

"A few years ago I had severe migraine headaches. A friend suggested I try yoga. After a few months of exercises, my headaches went away. Soon I got curious about Hindu spirituality. I found lots of wisdom in the talks at self-realization groups. I was especially interested in how meditation could reduce stress, since so many doctors think migraines are related to emotional turmoil.

"Now that I practice transcendental meditation for two periods each day, I'm much calmer. When I go to church I notice many Mass-goers fidgeting in the pews. I used to think that the Christian way was the only authentic way to God. Now I think there are many paths we could walk on."

Reflection and Prayer

The teaching of the Roman Catholic Church is that even though there are insights to be found in other religions, the fulness of truth has been given to our Church by the Holy Spirit. Other religions contain, along with certain truths, many errors and ambiguous practices. These can distract us from sheer graces given to us as Catholics.

You may or may not know about the meditative and contemplative practices of our tradition. Their purpose is to bring you into union with God, but as a side effect they also relieve stress and often bring physical healing as well. It would be well to explore this rich legacy before settling for a lesser form of meditation.

Different paths to the same goal? Consider some of the contrasts between most Asian beliefs and New Age beliefs, and the truths common to all three of the Jewish, Muslim, and Christian religions.

Our faith is monotheistic and has as its center an absolute personal creator God. By contrast, many religions of non-Western origin think of the highest divine as an impersonal energy, sometimes with demigods more like our angels or demons.

We believe that we were created in love by God and invited to live eternally as unique persons in union with him. By contrast, in most Eastern religions and those aspects of New Age teaching influenced by them, the conviction is that we have existed forever, going through successive reincarnations until such time as our self disappears, merged into an impersonal divine.

Because we believe in a personal Lord, we know ourselves to be obliged to obey him. In nontheistic religious systems (religions without a belief in a personal God), there is no notion of sin as a personal offense against God. Instead there is an emphasis on how ignorance leads to suffering.

Most importantly, we believe that Jesus came down from heaven to redeem us on a bloody cross. The wisdom figures of non-Christian Eastern religions, however, are more like our saints—holy, but not the unique Son of God.

It is not an offense to Jesus to engage in the physical side of yoga.

But it is an affront to meditate in a void when he longs for you to spend that time giving him your heart.

Openness to things new to you should never include anything demonic. Some people think that certain occult practices are now accepted by the Church. They are wrong. Consulting horoscopes and mediums, along with other exotic experiments, are warned against in the *Catechism*. (See 2115-2117 for the Scripture texts and reasoning behind such prohibitions. Also see the resource list at the end of this book.)

Here is a sample of how you might pray about the right path:

"O my Jesus, I have always loved you. I have no wish to offend you in anything. Thank you for any benefit I have gained from a practice of another religion. Show me whom to consult so I can learn about the deep spiritual life of saints and mystics. If, without knowing it, I have been open to anything tainted with demonic influence, please cleanse and deliver me."

∼ *Scripture for Meditation* ∼

There shall not be found among you any one who ... practices divination, a soothsayer or an augur, or a sorcerer, or a charmer, or a medium, or a wizard, or a necromancer. For whoever does these things is an abomination to the Lord.

DEUTERONOMY 18:10-12

I am the way, and the truth, and the life.

JOHN 14:6

Through him you have confidence in God, who raised him from the dead and gave him glory, so that your faith and hope are in God.

1 PETER 1:21

That which was from the beginning, which we have heard, which we have seen with our eyes, which we have looked upon and touched with our hands, concerning the word of life ...[we] proclaim to you the eternal life which was with the Father was made manifest to us ... so that you may have fellowship with us; and our fellowship is with the Father and with his Son Jesus Christ.

1 JOHN 1:1-3

Seven

Lord, I Never Thought I'd Feel Like This!

I sought the Lord, and he answered me, and delivered me from all my fears. Look to him, and be radiant.

PSALM 34:4-5

Do you think you can control your emotions the same way you press a button and the microwave heats up the food? Some of us practically grew up feeling overwhelmed, but for many, the onset of feelings we cannot control is a shock. Many of us don't know what to do with scary anxiety, intense anger, despairing disillusionment, or desperate loneliness. We want to wish these feelings away and be done with it, but they are stronger than we thought.

As we examine some of these emotions, we will find they have a logic of their own with causes not as mysterious as might appear. Best of all, we will find that God allows us to feel overwhelmed because he has plans not only to save us but to bring us to a better place than before. What we have to do is to hang on to the life raft, no matter how high the waves, and to let ourselves be lifted out by rescue crews both human and divine.

I Feel So Anxious Even When There's Nothing Wrong!

Unless the Lord builds the house, those who build it labor in vain.... It is in vain that you rise up early and go late to rest, eating the bread of anxious toil; for he gives to his beloved sleep.

PSALM 127:1-2

"The crisis counselor at the company I work for calls it free-floating anxiety. It is different from fear, because I don't know exactly what I'm anxious about. On the other hand, if I were feeling fear, she said, I could identify the cause. Some people are afraid of dogs; others of lightning. Many fear losing their jobs; others, losing their family members in accidents. Even though fear is always painful, it is different from feeling anxious without even knowing why.

"With me it started when we moved to another state. Since I was still in the same company and it was a promotion, I wasn't consciously upset about relocating. The city we moved to was one of my favorites on the sales route. My wife and children were happy about the change, which led to an upgrade in our standard of living.

"Just the same, five months into my new job I started waking up with a horrible anxious feeling, as if it were a premonition of something dreadful to come. At first I shrugged it off. But when it got more frequent and more intense, I mentioned it casually to a friend, who suggested I seek professional help."

Reflection and Prayer

Psychologists usually relate free-floating anxiety to repressed insecurity. The stressful pace of modern life, and the duties that compel many of us to forge ahead whatever the cost, often mask anxieties. It can take a trained psychotherapist to unearth the root causes of insecurity in an individual case.

Fears about a particular area of the country can be instilled in childhood. Dealing with new and unfamiliar personalities in management can trigger deep-seated anxiety about performance. There may be friends and neighbors in one town whose loving kindness swathes you in comfort. You took them for granted, but without them the difficulties in life seem overwhelming.

Whether or not you seek professional help for anxiety, you should know that it is never recommended to sit still brooding when anxiety floods your body and soul. Instead, you should engage in as much physical motion as possible and continue completing the work at hand, no matter how close you feel to collapse. Perhaps this is what Winston Churchill meant by his famous World War II proclamation to his people as the bombs were falling into their houses: "We have nothing to fear but fear itself!"

It is common to feel alone in the midst of anxiety. Because there is no clear reason for being anxious, even those close to you may be at a loss to understand. But there is One who is always with you. We know our Jesus understands when we remember his sweating blood in the Garden of Gethsemane. Who better to call on with passionate hope when the ground seems to be shaking under our feet?

Some of the most joyful holy people in the world went through periods of anxiety. Having been in this pit, they are especially good at helping others out of it.

A prayer to use during anxiety attacks might be this one:

"Dear Lord, I used to think of myself as strong. I hate feeling so weak. I beg you to take away these anxiety attacks. If there is a hidden cause I need to face, give me the courage to do so. Help me to surrender to you the areas in which I feel most insecure. With each tremor, let me breathe in your love as I repeat: 'Jesus, have mercy on me, a poor sinner.'"

～ Scripture for Meditation ～

Fill me with joy and gladness; let the bones which thou hast broken rejoice.

PSALM 51:8

We know that in everything God works for good with those who love him.

ROMANS 8:28

But God chose what is foolish in the world to shame the wise, God chose what is weak in the world to shame the strong, God chose what is low and despised in the world ... so that no human being might boast in the presence of God.... "Let him who boasts, boast of the Lord."

1 CORINTHIANS 1:27-31

I'm So Lonely!

His appearance was so marred, beyond human semblance.

ISAIAH 52:14

"I had a funny experience today. I went to the airport to pick up my beautiful teenage niece. She was coming for a few days to visit colleges in my city. As I waited around at the gate, no one talked to me, no one looked at me. If their glance happened to fall on me, they averted their eyes after a few seconds.

"Then, when my niece got off the plane, it seemed as if everyone stared at her. Even the strangers coming off the plane with her acted as if she were their bosom friend the way they hugged her good-bye. I remember now that when my mother became a widow, she used to say that her life was over. She felt old and ugly, the way I do now as a sixty-five-year-old widow myself.

"My daughter, who's forty and never married, also complains about how lonely she feels. Most of the people she knows from church are couples. They sometimes invite her to join them, but she feels like a sore thumb.

"It's as if maybe they think it's their duty to let singles come to their parties, but once she gets there she feels left out, sitting alone in a chair while others are talking up a storm all about their houses, their children, their grandchildren, and their vacation plans. I know she's dying to get married, but she just doesn't seem to be the type men go for."

Reflection and Prayer

There are so many kinds of loneliness in our world: the loneliness of parents after their children leave home; the loneliness of those who live by themselves by choice or circumstance; the loneliness of those separated, divorced, or bereaved. There is also the loneliness of those who live with others but in enmity or lacking a deep communion of hearts. There is loneliness when your love of Christ in the Church is not understood by those around you.

Being old and ugly is not a reason for anyone to feel worthless. If you feel that way, consider that the two most admired individuals of the twentieth century were old and ugly by Hollywood standards: Mother Teresa of Calcutta and Pope John Paul II! Instead of comparing yourself to, say, Marilyn Monroe and Nick Nolte, you should think when you look in the mirror: Every day in every way I am looking more like Mother Teresa or John Paul! Another antidote to feeling old and isolated is to meditate on the exquisite beauty of the resurrected body you will have in heaven and its closeness to millions of exalted believers.

We do not know exactly why some people are surrounded by loving family and friends while others are separate. Some who live alone would probably be better off giving up the relative peace of solitude for the dynamic interaction of living with others. There were communal saints and much more solitary ones, some choosing to be hermits as a way to be closer to God.

There is no guarantee in Scripture of popularity. Evidently Barabbas, a violent brigand, was admired more than Jesus by quite a number of people!

One thing guaranteed is that there will always be people for you to love. Coiling up in a cocoon of loneliness has never been the answer.

For instance, if you feel self-conscious at social occasions, you can talk to the person you see who seems the loneliest.

St. Thomas Aquinas said that you can only love yourself when you are a loving person. Think about it. When are you most joyful? When you love something or someone. Look at a sunset or a friend, and your heart expands; there is beauty of spirit in you whether you are young or old, physically attractive or wrinkled up.

Isn't it a more Christlike approach to each day not thinking about how much love you will get, but asking to whom you can show love? Jesus once told St. Teresa of Avila: "If you take care of my interests, I will take care of yours!"

On the deepest level, the greatest remedy for loneliness is to beg Jesus to open you to his love. We belong to him and he belongs to us. In his heart is total understanding, appreciation, and delight. If this prospect seems unreal to you, perhaps you need to take advantage of some different ways of prayer you will find described in chapter nine of this book.

You might pray about your loneliness in words like these:

"Dear God, you did not make us to be alone. If there are lonely people I could befriend, please bring me into contact with them. If there is anything in my character such as a critical, harsh, sullen, or melancholy spirit that alienates others, please heal me of these attitudes. Please send me the friends whose company will help me know you better. Give me hope in the total fellowship of love that, if I follow your will, I may one day enjoy in heaven."

∼ Scripture for Meditation ∼

Turn thou to me, and be gracious to me; for I am lonely and afflicted. Relieve the troubles of my heart, and bring me out of my distresses. Consider my affliction and my trouble, and forgive all my sins.

PSALM 25:16-18

I lie awake, I am like a lonely bird on the housetop.

PSALM 102:7

My beloved is mine and I am his.

SONG OF SOLOMON 2:16

For the law of the Spirit of life in Christ Jesus has set me free.... Those who live according to the flesh set their minds on the things of the flesh, but those who live according to the Spirit set their minds on the things of the Spirit.... But if Christ is in you,... your spirits are alive because of righteousness.... He who raised Christ Jesus from the dead will give life to your mortal bodies also through his Spirit who dwells in you.

ROMANS 8:2-11

I Feel So Let Down!

I kept my faith, even when I said, "I am greatly afflicted"; I said in my consternation, "Men are all a vain hope."

PSALM 116:10-11

"I never thought I would succumb to that malady people call 'burnout' when it came to pro-life activism. I was the first to join any initiative. First there were anti-abortion protest letters, then praying the rosary in front of the killing centers, giving talks at high schools, marches on Washington, counseling outreaches to pregnant women, and Operation Rescue. I was even dragged off to jail once, if only for a few hours.

"A feeling of disillusionment came with the failure of politicians who said they were personally against abortion to help us politically. That soured me on American democracy. Before *Roe v. Wade* I was a patriot. Now I am so ashamed of our country, I think about moving far away.

"What also drives me crazy is the apathy in our Church. If only every Christian who goes to church on Sundays would stand one hour a week in front of their neighborhood abortion clinic and pray, it would stop the killing! But they don't care. How can Catholics look up every Sunday at the man who died on the cross and think they should never make any sacrifice, even for the most innocent little beings in the whole world?

"Gradually I've stopped being so involved. It just seems hopeless."

Reflection and Prayer

There are many reasons for feeling let down. A sense of betrayal is one of the biggest. Personal betrayals will be addressed in the next chapter. Here our attention will be focused on social justice issues.

From Old Testament times, God's people were no strangers to injustice. In most cases they were the victims, but they also could be the perpetrators. After all, the first recorded sin after the Fall was a murder related to a seeming injustice: Cain and Abel.

When the odds are against you concerning injustice, the temptation to give up can be overwhelming. You may also fall into harsh judgment.

Read books and watch films about leaders of peaceful resistance such as Mohandas Gandhi and Martin Luther King, Jr. They can shame you by their remarkable forgiveness of their enemies. At the time of their protests they were considered fools. Now we can see much fruit from their labors.

What would you think if you were watching a movie about Jesus, and he suddenly stopped and cried out: "It's too much! There's no hope! Forget it! I'm going back to the life of a carpenter instead"?

To work for social justice, whether pro-life, defense of migrants, peace ministry, or some other cause, will seem hopelessly frustrating a lot of the time. Can you blame those who don't get involved for thinking they can do more good showing love in the family or their work rather than beating their heads against a seeming stone wall in public protest? And of course, a parent of many children may be giving a pro-life witness as influential as that of a picketer.

Just the same, after years of fighting for those victimized by injustice, you may need a break. If you have by nature a crusader type of personality, it will usually not work to sit still and do nothing. That could lead to cynicism and even despair. But sometimes a new method of coming against evil is needed that is less stressful. For instance, working on a written version of your best case for a cause, then distributing it in pamphlet form or on the Web, can be a quieter way to continue the battle.

Here is a prayer for a tired activist:

"Holy Spirit, it is you who put a fire into my heart for the defense of the victimized. You know all the sacrifices I have made through the years. Jesus didn't give up when even his closest disciples abandoned him. He died forgiving everyone responsible for that totally unjust crucifixion.

"Help me to forgive those who either are blind or just don't feel called to witness in the same way I do. In the case of blameworthy indifference, please wake them up. And if I have put anyone off by vehemence and judgment, forgive me. Give me fresh inspiration."

∼ Scripture for Meditation ∼

Why do the wicked live, reach old age, and grow mighty in power?... No rod of God is upon them.

JOB 21:7-9

Only in the Lord ... are righteousness and strength; to him shall come and be ashamed, all who were incensed against him. In the Lord all the offspring of Israel shall triumph and glory.

ISAIAH 45:24-25

Blessed are those who hunger and thirst for righteousness, for they shall be satisfied.

MATTHEW 5:6

We are witnesses to all that [Jesus] did both in the country of the Jews and in Jerusalem. They put him to death by hanging him on a tree; but God raised him on the third day and made him manifest.

ACTS 10:39-40

I'd Like to Kill My Boss!

Therefore they set taskmasters over them to afflict them with heavy burdens.

EXODUS 1:11

"I thought I'd love my job as a legal secretary. That was until the boss's son, Mr. Potter, came to take his father's place so his dad could retire. He had a great smile and lots of charm, but in other ways he was upsetting.

"He wanted us all to make work our whole life. I'm a fine worker when I'm at the office, but I really love my own time in the evening, especially for going out with my boyfriend. I prayed a long time for a guy as sweet and also as Christian as he is.

"Just before 5:00 P.M. each day, Mr. Potter began walking into our secretarial pool and asking who would stay and do overtime. He didn't say that promotion or getting fired was related to these requests, but pretty soon we saw the pattern. Any woman who stayed late regularly was given a raise. Those, like me, who never volunteered started getting the most pesky jobs during regular hours.

"One day Mr. Potter asked me whether he could take me out to lunch. I made a joke about having a boyfriend. 'Strictly professional,' he replied with a wink.

"After the drinks and appetizers, he said: 'You know, Cheryl, you're the best gal we have. I think you're too smart for secretarial work. I'd like to send you for special training so you can be a paralegal. Of course, those classes are in the evening. It's an intensive course, four nights a week for a month.'

"'I think I could manage that,' I said.

"The boss was delighted when I finished the course. He gave me a $10,000-a-year pay hike. When he announced the salary boost, he added: 'The hours are eight to six usually, but when we're busy you stay till 9:00 P.M. and come in on Saturday mornings.'

"I was so mad I wanted to grab the scissors on his desk and plunge them into his neck. How dare he manipulate me that way! I told him I'd have to think it over.

"I don't know what to do. The new job would mean working closely with him, and I can't stand his guts. Besides, I want to spend more, not less, time with my boyfriend, now my fiancé!"

Reflection and Prayer

Anger at the manipulative or exploitative techniques of bosses seems to have multiplied in our day. During an economic depression, people are so happy to get any job they can that they put up with a lot, especially in the way of overtime. But when jobs are more plentiful, people are less tolerant of such conditions.

Employees may also be mistreated through a boss's failure ever to show gratitude for work well done. Or an employer may present complicated tasks as simple, even though you don't understand them, and then blame you for failure. That situation is unjust and can make you furious.

If your deadlines cannot be met no matter how hard you try because of others' negligence—and management does nothing to remedy the situation—you will be frustrated. If the project is important, you may even be enraged.

In a world without original sin or subsequent sins, there would never be injustice in the workplace. After the Fall, however, it is unlikely that any place you work will be free from injustice. Bitter complaints to friends or coworkers let off steam, but don't change things much.

Some believe that as a Christian you are obliged to be meek and submissive even when there is objective wrong. It is true that some saints expressed their love for the meekness of the Lamb of God by offering all such frustrations up to God as a penance for their own and the sins of others. But other saints protested loudly against injustice.

In their social encyclicals the popes protested in the name of Christ against economic injustice. The right kind of trade unionism was encouraged. They took this position because of the extreme sufferings of those reduced to poverty by unfair wages. They also knew that there is a demeaning of the human person whenever someone is taken advantage of.

Feeling angry at injustice is a virtue, says St. Thomas Aquinas. But indulging in poisonous, fruitless anger is sinful. In cases of injustice, you need to pray for guidance to see whether there is something you can do to improve conditions.

If after speaking the truth with love to those responsible, you get no satisfaction, you can look into mediation or, as a last resort, legal action. Where there is little hope of change, you need to face the conflict between your need or desire to keep the job and the cross of dealing with the injustices of those in charge. In such situations it is important to come to peace.

Jesus promises peace to his followers. You can come to peace by accepting the fact that you don't have control over other people, even as you continue praying for change. You can also find peace by leaving, even if it means sacrificing the advantages of the position. These losses might be worth it to avoid chronic anger or constant battles.

Righteously angry people can pray in this manner:

"O Jesus, you know all my reasons for anger. You didn't condemn legitimate anger. You commend those who seek justice. But you don't want me so consumed by anger that I am unable to forgive and love those who harm me and others. Please give me the grace to forgive. Show me if there is anything I can change. If not, show me whether to stay or leave."

～Scripture for Meditation ～

The Lord is gracious and merciful, slow to anger and abounding in steadfast love.

PSALM 145:8

But I say to you that every one who is angry with his brother shall be liable to judgment; whoever insults his brother shall be liable to the council, and whoever says, "You fool!" shall be liable to the hell of fire.

MATTHEW 5:22

Be angry but do not sin; do not let the sun go down on your anger, and give no opportunity to the devil.

EPHESIANS 4:26-27

I Just Want to Give Up!

Let us conduct ourselves becomingly as in the day, not in revel-
ing and drunkenness, not in debauchery and licentiousness, not
in quarreling and jealousy. But put on the Lord Jesus Christ,
and make no provision for the flesh, to gratify its desires.

ROMANS 13:13-14

"It's too hard. I've tried to be a good Catholic, but I just can't overcome sexual sins. When my wife divorced me suddenly after twenty-five years of marriage, it felt worse than death.

"After a few years of hoping she'd come back, we tried for an annulment, but there were insufficient grounds. She got married again outside the Church. At that point I stopped fighting it.

"I need a woman to feel alive. You wouldn't believe how many lonely, divorced women there are who want a sexual relationship but not marriage. They've also been burned.

"I still go to Sunday Mass and sometimes confession, between girl-friends. The priest suggested a support group or even Sexaholics Anonymous, a group for those who can't control their sexual fantasies and drives. Who's he kidding? No way I'd sit around talking about that stuff with strangers."

Reflection and Prayer

Satan is the father of lies (see Jn 8:44). The idea that you will dry up or die if you don't have sex is one of his favorites. In spite of temptation, regret, and sadness at times at the deprivation, millions of men and women throughout the ages have been as content as anyone can be in this valley of tears without the sexual pleasures married people enjoy.

If you believe the divorce statistics, in spite of the availability of sexual intercourse, happiness in marriage is not the rule. Most conflict and disappointment in marriage does not come from sexual problems. More often extreme incompatibilities are symptoms of a lack of communication.

It is the teaching of the Church that sexual activity outside of marriage is sinful. Sexual contact should be a beautiful life-giving expression of the love of spouses. It is a gift of God, not a right the absence of which justifies sin. Casual relationships may be exciting, but they will leave you and your partners with holes in your hearts.

Readiness to give up on struggling with sin is unfortunately all too common. It reaches a peak in the case of addictions of all kinds, the sinfulness of which varies with degree and circumstances. Addictions can take many forms: alcoholism, drug abuse, overeating, smoking, gambling, over-spending, out-of-control sexual fantasies and actions.

If you see that your sins are not rare capitulations to weakness, but rather a pattern that you cannot overcome no matter how much you pray for the grace and receive absolution, you may need to humble yourself enough to participate in counseling or a twelve-step program for healing. Programs designed for childhood victims of parents with such addictions can be helpful as well, not so much to get rid of your sins as to help you understand traits in your character that puzzle and hurt you.

There are two ways to "give up." One is to stop struggling and just indulge in addictive excess to the hilt. The other is to "give up" trying to be victorious through willpower alone. You must admit you are powerless over your addiction. Then you must totally surrender to God to help you avoid near occasions of sin through the supporting friendship of others God has helped work through the same problems.

A prayer for those overwhelmed by sin:

"Dear God, I am powerless over my sin. Fill me with your love so that I don't seek comfort in disordered ways. Give me the humility to find the human help I need. Deliver me from the lies of Satan."

∼ Scripture for Meditation ∼

Wash yourselves; make yourselves clean; remove the evil of your doings from before my eyes; cease to do evil, learn to do good.

ISAIAH 1:16-17

There is joy before the angels of God over one sinner who repents.

LUKE 15:10

We all once lived in the passions of our flesh, following the desires of body and mind, and so were by nature children of wrath, like the rest of mankind. But God, who is rich in mercy, out of the great love with which he loved us, even when we were dead through our trespasses, made us alive together with Christ.

EPHESIANS 2:3-5

Put off your old nature which belongs to your former manner of life and is corrupt through deceitful lusts, and be renewed in the spirit of your minds, and put on the new nature, created after the likeness of God in true righteousness and holiness.

EPHESIANS 4:22-24

In your struggle against sin you have not yet resisted to the point of shedding your blood.

HEBREWS 12:4

Resist the devil and he will flee from you.

JAMES 4:7

Eight

God, Help Me Love Those I Don't Like at All!

A gentle tongue is a tree of life.

PROVERBS 15:4

The two greatest commandments are to love God and to love your neighbor as yourself. He said *love*—not "act as if you loved"! St. John of the Cross wrote that in the evening of life, you will be judged by love. The great Christian novelist Fyodor Dostoevsky admitted, however, that as much as he loved his neighbor in the abstract as a brother, a man had only to blow his nose in an unpleasant way for love to turn to disgust!

It is hard enough to love strangers who exhibit annoying or evil traits. But how much harder it is to love those close to us when they hurt us to the point where we feel dislike and even hate! These wounds can come to us from parents, siblings, boyfriends or girlfriends, spouses, even priests.

A common thread here is the sense of injustice. I tried so hard to be good; I did so much; and look what they did to me! We long for the forgiveness of those we have hurt, but find it so hard to forgive those who hurt us. How often in our conflicts with those who have disappointed us do we wind up having won a battle but losing the war!

At some periods of our lives we may find that so many dear friends

153

have betrayed us, we think there is no such thing as love. We need to remember that given the realities of our fallen nature, any love we can give or receive is a kind of miracle. At such times the following reflection of the German Catholic writer Gertrud von Le Fort is helpful.

A disillusioned young priest is so incensed at the injustices he sees in society and church that he is ready to give up. An older priest says: "Justice you will find in hell. In heaven is mercy. On earth is the cross."

How happy are they who expect the cross, and then rejoice at all the happy surprises and gifts that come from the hands of the Father! Relationships based on merciful forgiveness last the longest, as we continue to love others in spite of failings, to love ourselves in spite of failings, and to open to the precious if flawed love of others for us.

The Children I Sacrificed So Much for Are Kicking Me in the Teeth!

Thou dost rebuke the insolent ... who wander from thy commandments; take away from me their scorn and contempt, for I have kept thy testimonies.

PSALM 119:21-22

"My daughter came home from college for Easter vacation. When I reminded her to get ready for the Good Friday service, she said she wasn't going. 'Why not?' I asked. She had always gone with me to Mass on Sundays and seemed to really get into the special holy days of Passion Week.

"'You're not going to like this, Mom, but I just don't believe all that anymore. I feel like you tried so hard to get us to be like you that we didn't have any choice. Now I'm eighteen, and it's time to decide for myself.'

"Since going to college my beautiful girl has become like a different person. She rarely calls us. When she's home for vacations she hardly talks to her dad or to me. She just runs with her friends instead. Whenever I say anything religious, she rolls her eyes at her younger brother, who also now says he won't go to church.

"My husband says not to worry, it's just a phase, but I know plenty of other families of strong Catholics where the kids left the church and haven't come back even in their thirties. I feel as if I have a dagger in my heart when I see my two children staying out late Saturday night and then getting up at noon Sunday, just as if they never even were Christians!"

Reflection and Prayer

You feel you have given your children the best, sometimes at great sacrifice, and they seem to throw it all out—it's a common situation that causes many parents bitter sorrow. Your child may have dropped out of school, adopted values opposite to your own, or lost the faith. Where previously your love for your child was full of admiration and praise, now your love survives mostly as pain.

You cannot pretend to be glad when the young ones abandon truths and values you know to be necessary for their happiness and salvation. Sorrow, yes. But bitterness, no!

Why not? Because bitterness is tinged with despair. You need to have hopeful trust that they will one day love the very things they have discarded in their youthful rebellion. Jesus suffered with you when in the agony in the garden he took on all the sin in the world. He wants you to believe that through his loving grace, your children will one day come back, like the Prodigal Son. If you become too bitter, they might not see an open door.

Some young people never depart from parental norms and values, but they are few. Even though it is so distressing, it seems to be part of the growth of teens and young adults to try to find out for themselves the truths of the faith you wanted them to have as a legacy.

A book about rebellious children by Rudolf Dreikurs and Pearl Cassel, *Discipline Without Tears,* offers a series of questions that might be applicable to your older family members as well. When a child is sassy and adversarial, is it because he or she wants special attention? Is the child trying to become the boss? Is there a desire to hurt you because he or she has been hurt in the past? Is there a desire to be left alone?

Most likely a young person who refuses to join in family customs and religious practices is struggling for autonomy. If there have been wounds in the past, opposition may be a way of asking you to show your love not by arguing but by reassurance. A sarcastic comment such as "I guess Jesus could have stayed in bed on Good Friday, too" might sound snappy, but it will usually cause defensiveness.

A better type of response might be: "You know I wish you'd go with us to church, but I'm prepared to keep loving you just as you are." Offering up the suffering while giving your child space to be alone is sometimes the only option.

Prayer for a child on the wrong path:

"Dear God, only you know all the prayers I've sent up for my child to be close to you all his or her life. Please never give up on my son or daughter. Help me not to show despair by anxiety and nagging. Let my young adult children see in the love shining in my eyes a reflection of your love for everything good in them and hope for all that will be after their conversions."

~ Scripture for Meditation ~

I kept my faith, even when I said, "I am greatly afflicted."

PSALM 116:10

A soft tongue will break a bone.

PROVERBS 25:15

Speaking the truth in love, we are to grow up in every way into him who is the head, into Christ.

EPHESIANS 4:15

My Parents Criticize Me All the Time!

Forget your people and your father's house.

PSALM 45:10

"I'm thirty-five, but my father and mother still can't stop telling me what to do. If I don't obey them and then things don't work out, they ridicule me with 'I told you so.' I'm sick of it. I dread family visits. Of course, everything my older brother does is perfect. It's been like that since we were kids.

"The visit starts with my dad jabbing my stomach. 'Why don't you get rid of that tire, son?'

"Then comes from Mom, 'The third baby is coming soon; when are you getting a bigger house?' Or 'I notice Clare looks worn out. Are you helping her enough?'

"My wife and I take bets on how soon Dad will say, 'If you're going to the trouble of a barbecue, you should get a better grade of meat.' This time it was 'Your brother said there's an opening at his company. Why don't you try for it? Your job is a dead end!'

"Once I tried to explain to them that we just didn't have the same values. I don't care about looking trim or having a big house. My wife and I get along fine. We think it's kind of Christian to care more about our kids than our status.

"But they can't let go. By the time they go home, I feel like a failure. Why can't they just stop it?"

Reflection and Prayer

For some parents, a child is always a child in need of helpful advice. I know of one ninety-year-old woman who told her seventy-year-old daughter to be careful about marrying a widower who might not be intellectual enough for her! Because of differing values, your parents may think that if they were living as you are, they would be unhappy. So they deduce that you must be unhappy and in need of their wisdom to improve your life.

Psychologists say that it is a good idea to expect people to remain as they are rather than always hoping they will change. Unless your parents have a reason of their own to discover the limitations of their values as compared to yours, they will probably continue to criticize your ways. You have a choice: You can allow them to make you feel inferior, or you can use their advice as an opportunity to reassert your more Christian values for your family.

It is probably better not to hope for understanding, only to be disappointed time after time. You can pray that God will show your parents a better way. You can consciously praise God that you are doing well in terms of what really counts.

If you hate it when your parents seem to want you to be a clone of themselves instead of being yourself, you may need to ask how well you're doing with your own children in that respect. Are you careful that the majority of your input isn't critical? If someone made a tape recording of all your communications with your children over the course of a day, would the majority of those communications be affirming or at least neutral? Never pass by someone you love without showing it, the Catholic philosopher Dietrich von Hildebrand used to say.

Here is the type of prayer you can use if you feel low after family visits:

"Dear Father God, I know that you are the Father who understands me totally and affirms what is good in me and my family. Thank you for all the ways my human father helped me to grow. [Recall his virtues in this respect.] I feel hurt when my dad and mom fail to appreciate me. Help us grow closer as time goes on.

"Meanwhile, help me to take any insensitive remarks more lightly. Thank you for the insights you have given us into the meaning of life and your help to be who we are. Help me to be tolerant of the ways our children are different from us."

∼ Scripture for Meditation ∼

Help your father in his old age, and do not grieve him as long as he lives; even if he is lacking in understanding, show forbearance.

SIRACH 3:12-13

Fathers, do not provoke your children, lest they be discouraged.
COLOSSIANS 3:21

Have no anxiety about anything, but in everything by prayer and supplication with thanksgiving let your requests be made known to God. And the peace of God, which passes all understanding, will keep your hearts and your minds in Christ Jesus.
PHILIPPIANS 4:6-7

I Can't Trust the Person of the Opposite Sex I Love(d) the Most!

What therefore God has joined together, let no man put asunder.

MATTHEW 19:6

"Our marriage was different. We started out as just friends for years doing youth ministry together. We loved each other's souls first. We got to see each other under stressful working conditions, sometimes staying up night after night on retreats talking to troubled teens.

"We got married five years after we met. When the babies started coming, we got a lot busier, with less time to go to Mass together or pray at home, since my husband had to take a job with long business commutes. After the second baby, I was so exhausted we decided to use contraceptives for a few years until I got my strength back.

"Last week a friend of mine said she saw my husband in the middle of the day going into a motel room with another woman. I was shocked. When I asked him about it, sure that he would deny it all, he admitted he was having an affair with one of the other salespeople from work.

"'Why?' I asked, crying. He said he didn't know, but it didn't mean anything to him really. It wouldn't happen again. I'm devastated. How can I ever trust him again?"

Reflection and Prayer

True love is not just a matter of attraction, common values, or ideals. As von Hildebrand wrote, love is a response to the unique preciousness of the other. The Holy Father writes about a configuration of persons made for each other such that the personhood of the other matches yours. This leads you to want to give yourself to him or her.

Because of the power of such special love, you can readily think that it is absolute in the sense of flawless. But no matter how beautiful the love, human beings are full of imperfections, character defects, and sinful tendencies. You may be attracted to someone other than your spouse, not necessarily because your marriage is on the rocks, but sometimes just because of you feel tired, a little bored, or eager to test your own virility or sexual magnetism. Yet the relationships, short or long, that develop from such shallow motives can in no way compare to the deep love you have for a person with whom you are bonded in sacramental marriage.

Some Catholic philosophers have noted, by the way, that a man may consciously choose to go for contraceptives within a marriage but unconsciously feel it as a blow to his manhood, and then seek out other women as a compensation. As with anything that the Holy Spirit has taught the Church to prohibit, there are usually many good reasons for the prohibition.

The great pain you experience if your boyfriend or girlfriend, fiancé, or spouse is unfaithful does not excuse you from practicing the mercy Jesus wants you to show. In fact, your marriage could become much stronger when it is shorn of illusions and is based instead on a clear understanding of the temptations and weaknesses of the other. This could be a time for a reevaluation of your marital lives. You could experience a renewal of your relationship after confession of sins against each other, including the sin of withholding your fertility from each other through contraception. (See the resources listed at the end of the book for information on how natural family planning differs from contraception.)

What if a spouse's infidelity is not a one-time sin, but a pattern? What if the sin is leading a couple toward separation and divorce? Can men and women stay together in a Christian marriage if one or both are breaking their vows consistently?

Such is a tragic state of affairs, not only for the couple, but also for the children. Sometimes a canon lawyer will see in one or both spouses a psychologically addicted condition that made their vows to each other null—hence the term "annulment." But often the right kind of marriage counseling from a spiritual mentor or psychologist can help bring about conversion, confession, absolution, and a renewal of the marriage.

In cases where separation and divorce are chosen and remarriage is not an option according to the deliberations of the canon lawyers, what will happen to the brokenhearted spouse? When the human bridegroom or bride fails, you have all the more reason to cling to Jesus, the bridegroom of your soul. Mystically united to him, with greater fervor than before your rejection, you will let him teach you how to love others with tenderness rather than a thirst based on illusions of perfection. Along with this heavy cross, God will send you the human love that you need from family, friends, and the Church.

A way for a rejected person to pray:

"Jesus, more beautiful than any human lover, I run into your arms, crushed and battered. Please help me forgive the weaknesses and sins of the one who hurt me so much. If there is a path to reconciliation based on forgiveness, please open my heart to walk in it. If the path is permanently closed off, help me to avoid hatred and anguish. Let the wound in my heart be a conduit from which the living waters of your love will flow from me to others equally in need."

∼ *Scripture for Meditation* ∼

I will make you lie down in safety. And I will betroth you to me for ever; I will betroth you to me in righteousness and in justice, in steadfast love, and in mercy. I will betroth you to me in faithfulness; and you shall know the Lord.

HOSEA 2:18-20

Forgive us our debts, as we also have forgiven our debtors.

MATTHEW 6:12

He who has the bride is the bridegroom.

JOHN 3:29

Therefore, my beloved ... work out your own salvation with fear and trembling; for God is at work in you, both to will and to work for his good pleasure.

PHILIPPIANS 2:12-13

My Brothers and Sisters in Ministry Won't Cooperate

The love of Christ controls us.

2 CORINTHIANS 5:14

"For many years I was part of the St. Vincent de Paul Society in my parish. I disagreed with the leader. It seemed we were mostly just giving out stuff without really getting to know the people so we could help in other ways.

"When my wife and I moved to another state, it turned out that they needed a St. Vincent de Paul leader in one of the parishes. I would have free rein to do it as I thought fit.

"I insisted on having an office in the parish hall. At our first meeting I told the group I wanted to have visits to homes, a soup kitchen once a week, and more spiritual outreach to those we served. They were happy to do it. When the house across the street from the church went up for sale, our group agreed to combine our discretionary funds to buy the house so we could start a shelter for women and children at risk.

"To my surprise, the parish council nixed the shelter. They said they were afraid of insurance issues. What if a kid or a raging father from one of the families in the shelter hurt a child at our parish school?

"I was so upset. What kind of Christians do we have at our church? Here we were ready to foot the bill at quite a personal sacrifice, and they were looking for ways to avoid the slightest possibility of legal troubles. Some good Samaritans!

"I feel so angry that I'm thinking of quitting the ministry. With all the free time I'll have, I'll get to know these parish council members even better at the watering hole of the golf course!"

Reflection and Prayer

"Anything worth doing is worth doing badly," quipped the English Catholic writer G.K. Chesterton. If every zealous member of the Church community had waited to minister until he or she had not only a perfect blueprint but also perfect circumstances and perfect agreement among fellow Christians, little would have been done in the twenty centuries since the resurrection of Christ. If you read the Acts of the Apostles and the Letters in the New Testament, you will find ample evidence of conflict, rivalry, and just messiness in the attempts of the apostles and disciples to spread the gospel and to help the needy. Come to think of it, even when Jesus walked the earth, his followers disagreed!

It is wonderful to try to do your best as a disciple of one of the greatest saints ever canonized, St. Vincent de Paul. Reaching out to those in need in the most effective ways possible is a sign of your love of God and neighbor. The Holy Father, however, emphasizes in his letters that we need not so much new programs as more holy people initiating them. It is not the program that will save; it is the presence of Christ emanating from your hearts.

With regard to love for the poor, your hearts are in the right place. But what about love for your brothers and sisters on the parish council? Is there some hasty or harsh judgment on your part? When the Lord builds the foundation of "the house" (see Ps 127:1), it is with the mortar of love, not the bile of sarcasm, that the bricks stick together.

Often months or years later you may find out that a criticism leveled against some project was justified. When those in our parish who are also praying to the Holy Spirit for guidance bring an objection forward, it may be part of God's will for you and your group to meet that problem head on rather than pouring contempt on those who disagree with you. And if you go off sulking in frustration about one project, what of all those needy people your other works would have helped?

A general prayer for the parish may combine your frustrated zeal with temperance:

"Come, Holy Spirit, enlighten us as we give our all for the ministry Jesus began. Please give us the wisdom and prudence to see how to overcome any objections to our plans. Especially touch the hearts of any in our parish who are blind to the sufferings of the poor. If we are in the wrong about an action, give us humility to be open to suggestions. Keep us from discouragement when only part of our program can be initiated at this time."

∼ Scripture for Meditation ∼

Unless the Lord builds the house, those who build it labor in vain.
PSALM 127:1

Blessed are the peacemakers, for they shall be called sons of God.
MATTHEW 5:9

For I was hungry and you gave me food.

MATTHEW 25:35

Now the works of the flesh are ... enmity, strife, jealousy, anger ... dissension, party spirit.... But the fruit of the Spirit is love, joy, peace, patience, kindness, goodness, faithfulness, gentleness, self-control.

GALATIANS 5:19-23

My Priest Isn't Holy!

And Peter remembered the word of the Lord, how he had said to him, "Before the cock crows today, you will deny me three times." And he went out and wept bitterly.

LUKE 22:61-62

"I was new in the parish when my husband was rushed to the hospital with a severe asthma attack. While they were giving him treatment in the emergency ward, I asked for the chaplain. Since she turned out to be a non-Catholic who could give advice but not anointing, I called the parish.

"The message said the priest wasn't in but could be reached on his cell phone in an emergency. I called that number and left a message, but he never came. Fortunately, my husband survived the crisis.

"Later, when I found out that it was the priest's bridge night, I could hardly believe it. I never talked to him about it, but I started noticing other things. For example, when a group of us from the Legion of Mary wanted to have twenty-four-hour eucharistic adoration, he refused.

"He said it was because there wouldn't be enough people coming, so Jesus would be left alone, which was not allowed. Others thought he just didn't want to take the trouble to administer Benediction before reposing the Blessed Sacrament. It could interfere with sleeping in till the last moment before the morning Mass.

"I don't know what to think. I've heard worse things about this priest, but I don't want to go on what could just be gossip. Still, I wonder.

"It's making it hard to go to his Masses. Every time he's not back from a vacation when he said he would be, I wonder whether he's going AWOL on us. I'm thinking seriously of going to another church for Mass, even though it's an hour away."

Reflection and Prayer

What might be going on in the soul of a priest who is lacking in zeal? Could he have become exhausted from being the only priest in the parish? Could he feel depressed, so that he thinks his need for recreation is much greater than any parishioner's need for emergency ministry? Could he have become convinced that Jesus will take care of his flock when he is too tired to do it?

How often do you pray for your priest or do penance for him? Do you consider that at one time in his life he had to be on fire for the Lord to decide to make such a hard sacrifice? You might be surprised to know how many times your priest wanted to leave but overcame the temptation out of love for Jesus and for his mystical body, including you.

Some ardent lay Catholics make it a point to affirm their priests every single day for everything good they do. When they have a need that only a priest can fulfill, they try to work around any resistance by starting small. For example, Eucharistic adoration one morning a week with petitions for your priest on a day you know he is available could be a better start than asking immediately for twenty-four hours.

Chipping in for the money to send your priest on a pilgrimage can bring graces of renewal. Befriending him by inviting him to dinner or leisure activities can help. Sometimes the priest can be the loneliest person in the parish.

In the meantime, we have to realize that there is no line in the creed that says, "I believe in Fr. Jones." He is a sinner just like ourselves with as much of a struggle to stay in his vocation as many of the rest of us have had staying in a marriage or a frustrating job. After all, our first pope, St. Peter, betrayed the Lord three times!

On the other hand, if there is a parish within your range where you would find much more help in your journey to holiness, you have a right to go there. A strong reason for such a choice would be if your priest is not just lacking in fervor and zeal about some matters, but also proclaiming false teaching or practice from the pulpit or in other contexts.

In the Old Testament as well as the New, you find incredible examples of forgiveness, such as Joseph's forgiving the brothers who tried to kill him out of jealousy, or David's forgiving Saul for trying to kill him in battle in spite of his own loyalty. You need to forgive your priest for any action or omission that hurt you personally. You also should avoid gossiping about his faults and especially avoid gloating maliciously over new instances of his shortcomings. If you tend toward resentment and gossip, you need to confess these sins against charity.

A prayer to say for a lax priest:

"Dear Jesus and Mary, I know how much you love your priests. Thank you for all the years of ministry of my priest. Thank you for every Mass he has celebrated, every sacrament he has administered. Thank you especially for using him in confession in the forgiving of my sins.

"Please renew his spirit so that he can model your sacrificial love for us and lead us in our piety. Forgive me for any detraction in letting others in on faults or actions of his they may not have known about."

~ *Scripture for Meditation* ~

For no man living is righteous before thee.

PSALM 143:2

He who goes about as a talebearer reveals secrets, but he who is trustworthy in spirit keeps a thing hidden.

PROVERBS 11:13

He who forgives an offense seeks love, but he who repeats a matter alienates a friend.

PROVERBS 17:9

If a man has a hundred sheep, and one of them has gone astray, does he not leave the ninety-nine on the hills and go in search of the one that went astray? And if he finds it, truly, I say to you, he rejoices over it more than over the ninety-nine that never went astray.

MATTHEW 18:12-13

How Can I Love Someone
Who Abused My Child?

And God will wipe away every tear from their eyes.

REVELATION 7:17

"'That can't be true. Your grandfather would never do such a thing. You must be imagining something ... exaggerating.' That's how I reacted when my daughter told me about her horrible memories.

"'When the memory came up during the healing retreat, I also thought it couldn't be true,' my daughter said. 'The priest asked us to recall any time that anyone molested us when we were children. I suddenly remembered how Grandpa used to put his hand up my skirt and pet me up there when he took me to the movies.

"'I hadn't thought about it for years. The priest said that often a memory is shameful, and then it is repressed. Just the same it can lead to fears, revulsion, or sometimes promiscuity later on in life.'

"'Still,' I persisted, 'are you sure he didn't just put his hand on your knee?'

"'I had doubts, too,' she said, 'so I checked with Chantal. Remember how we used to take turns going with Grandpa to the movies during that year when you were so sick after the baby was born? She immediately remembered the same thing. She thought it had something to do with the way she's obsessed with sex now.'"

Reflection and Prayer

Finding out that a member of the family or some other trusted person such as a teacher, sister, priest, or brother was engaged in the past in sinful sexual activity, especially with an innocent child, makes you feel confused, furious, and disillusioned. The closer the victimizer is to you, the worse you feel.

In the case of an abuse continuing in the present, you need to take immediate action, even to the point of reporting the matter to the law.

When finding out about past sins, sometimes Christians want to conceal the problem. There may be wisdom in keeping such matters secret from strangers. But most often those in the family have a sense of something wrong in the present or past. They have often been affected in unconscious ways. Talking about it privately with the victimizer may be the beginning of healing, not only for those directly involved, but also for others whose emotions have been twisted by those secret sins.

Relying on your own wisdom about how to deal with sexual sins such as incest, rape, or homosexual abuse is not a good idea. Professional experts in the field of psychological and spiritual counseling, many of whom are Christians, have years of experience helping victims. The impulse to hide such sins, partly out of family pride, should not keep you from finding help.

Truth, even tragic truth, is meant to set us free. If, as a result of healing, the person violated is able to forgive, she or he may be able lovingly to confront the victimizer and come to reconciliation. If you are the parent of the one abused and the abuser is your parent, there is an even greater need for healing. Even when the perpetrator denies his or her acts out of shame and fear, a process has been started that could lead, at least, to death-bed repentance and confession.

The mother of the holy girl St. Maria Goretti was given the grace to forgive the man who killed her daughter while trying to rape her, even before he came to the mother in repentance. Years later, as a penitent, this man stood in the square of St. Peter's watching the girl he wanted to rape being canonized!

You might want to send up a prayer such as this:

"Lord, have mercy on my family and friends. Please heal the wounds that came from sexual abuse in the past. When I think of the victimizer, keep me from disturbing images. Instead let me gently place him or her into your arms. I offer to you now the pain I am feeling, for the salvation of the soul of the abuser."

∼ Scripture for Meditation ∼

He took hold of her, and said to her, "Come, lie with me, my sister." She answered him, "No, my brother, do not force me; for such a thing is not done in Israel; do not do this wanton folly.... But he would not listen to her; and being stronger than she, he forced her, and lay with her.... Tamar put ashes on her head ... and went away, crying aloud as she went.

2 SAMUEL 13:11-19

Whoever causes one of these little ones who believe in me to sin, it would be better for him if a great millstone were hung around his neck and he were thrown into the sea.

MARK 9:42

If your brother sins, rebuke him, and if he repents, forgive him;
and if he sins against you seven times in the day, and turns to
you seven times, and says, "I repent," you must forgive him.

LUKE 17:3-4

Nine

An Hour Together With the Lord

"Could you not watch with me one hour?"

MATTHEW 26:40

When you hear the phrase "holy hour," you may be thinking only of time spent in the church in front of the Blessed Sacrament either in the Tabernacle or exposed in a monstrance for adoration. It is wonderful to make a holy hour in the real presence of Jesus in that way, but you can also spend a deep time of communion with Jesus at home, on a walk, in your car, or anywhere.

I cannot think of a single saint who became holy without long times of prayer in addition to Mass, along with other formal prayers such as the liturgy of the hours or the rosary. Whenever he experiences overwhelming temptations to sin, one of my friends rides on a motorcycle to churches even hours away where they have the Blessed Sacrament exposed. He says that he just stays there until the grace comes to continue on the right path!

In this chapter, I will focus on how you can use your holy hour—whether it's every day or once a week—not so much as a means to overcome sin, but rather as a way to receive the comfort and strength Jesus wants to give you as you try to cope with your problems.

"Draw near to God and he will draw near to you" (Jas 4:8).

Sometimes when we feel just awful, we think that if God wants us to keep going he'll have to come to us big time, maybe with an apparition! Sometimes God does answer such desperate prayers with a sudden vision, but usually he seems to want to draw us into his heart through the means he has made available to all in his mystical body, the Church.

In the religious community where I live as a consecrated widow, we have adoration every weekday from 5:00 to 6:00 P.M. Even though Holy Mass is where Christ is most present in the universe, and I participate frequently in the Mass for that reason, I find that my holy hour is the time when I can sit still and let him come to me in the places of my heart where I am most vulnerable, wounded, and just confused. After the hymns of adoration, I like just to lay it all out to God something like this:

"Dear Jesus, here you are. Now your body is center stage in the monstrance, and I feel small as I crouch on the floor gazing at you. I feel I am so weak that I can hardly go on in life. I am so tired. I realize that this is just where you want me, small and open, so that you can be my healing and strength; so that by filling me, you can be love for those around me."

Then I give Jesus my problems and wait in the silence for insight. Sometimes the Holy Spirit gives me what seem to be clear marching orders for that day or wisdom about future decisions. But often I hear something more general, such as this: "If you were smaller, not thinking you had to be great, you could get through a day better. Small people are more patient." Or: "If you saw life less as a burden and more as a dance, you would be happier."

When I open Scripture or other spiritual reading during holy hour, I tend to hear the message more personally. Sometimes I put my name into each verse. "Ronda, I have called you by name, thou art mine."

Or, "Because you are sons [a daughter], God has sent the Spirit of his Son into our hearts [your heart], crying, 'Abba! Father!' So through God you [Ronda] are no longer a slave but a son [daughter], and if a son [daughter] then an heir" (Gal 4:6-7).

In the case of tough decisions, such as those involving my vocation or family, I find that I can discern better during a holy hour. I seem more willing to admit that no matter how urgent it may seem, a tempting choice has to be wrong if it leaves me rattled, depressed, and miserable. When a choice is challenging but requires sacrifices I might not be disposed to take on, I find it a sign that I should do it anyway when I can feel the bubbling up of fresh energy.

A holy hour is a wonderful time to work out what memories involving sin and guilt would benefit from a general confession. For example, when I hear that someone I love has died, I like to bring to the sacrament of reconciliation any sins I committed concerning that person. Sometimes I like to say, "I am making a general confession of all the times I failed to trust in God, especially the last time." Then I go into detail about the last one.

Best of all, I find, are times during interior personal prayer when I am feeling crushed by loneliness. I realize I have to let go and let God, because there is no way I can keep close to me someone I depend on for desperately needed support. If I sit long enough in the presence of Jesus, he will always show me that his love, though not visible, is greater than any purely human love. I will leave feeling cherished even if tearful.

Once I was sharing with a holy contemplative nun certain words of love Jesus had told me in my heart during prayer. "Jesus doesn't talk to me," she said. I thought she meant she was envious of my prayer life. I was mistaken.

"He speaks to me in silence," she explained. Silence between lovers is sometimes more eloquent than words. If you are more like that nun than like me, don't feel you've been cheated. Ask the Holy Spirit to show you how Jesus speaks to you in the silence—for example, in the face of a flower, or the magnificence of the ocean, or the charm of a baby. These gifts can be brought to your holy hour for your thanksgiving time.

When you are distracted during holy hour, it is good to read a few lines from Scripture or spiritual books and then meditate on them. A good way to come into a balance in your relationship to God is to divide your holy hour into time for praise, another time for thanksgiving, another for contrition, and then some minutes for petition. Each way of prayer brings out different and essential elements in the spiritual life. If you have not experienced it, you may want to ask a friend who has done so how you could open yourself to charismatic prayer or the Jesus prayer of the heart.

In the resource section you will find readings explaining the history of eucharistic adoration and some on personal contemplative prayer.

Ten

In the Company of Mary, the Angels, and the Saints

They went up to the upper room, where they were staying, Peter and John and James and Andrew, Philip and Thomas, Bartholomew and Matthew, James the son of Alphaeus and Simon the Zealot and Judas the son of James. All these with one accord devoted themselves to prayer, together with the women and Mary the mother of Jesus.

ACTS 1:13-14

All generations will call me blessed.

LUKE 1:48

In heaven their angels always behold the face of my Father who is in heaven.

MATTHEW 18:10

[The saints'] intercession is their most exalted service to God's plan. We can and should ask them to intercede for us and for the whole world.

Catechism of the Catholic Church (2683)

If you have any doubts about the place of Mary, the angels, and the saints in the life of a Catholic believer, the best place to go for brief, solid, and clear teaching is the *Catechism of the Catholic Church*. If you go through the index searching for these topics, you will find exactly what you are looking for, and in the sections indicated you will find references to Scripture as well as to more extensive Magisterial teaching.

One of the greatest of non-Christian mystics, Plotinus, thought of departure from life on earth as going from "the alone to the alone." How different from the Catholic expectation! In heaven, where we long to go, we will certainly be loved in a personal and unique manner, but we will not be alone. We will adore our Lord and Savior within his mystical body, united in joy with those of the same longing: family, friends, and that celestial "squad" that cheered us on—Mary, the angels, and the saints.

During your difficult journey through life, you need as much help as you can get. That is why Catholics have always put trust in their heavenly mother, guardian angels, and favorite saints. In the list of resources at the end of this book you will find references to books of theology and prayer about Mary, the angels, and the saints. In this chapter you will find some of the most beloved prayers asking Mary's intercession, as well as a list of some saints who are patrons for the most common professions or circumstances.

Hail, Mary

Hail Mary, full of grace,
the Lord is with thee.
Blessed art thou among women,
and blessed is the fruit of thy womb, Jesus.
Holy Mary, Mother of God,
pray for us sinners,
now and at the hour of our death. Amen.

Salve Regina

Hail, Holy Queen, Mother of Mercy;
Hail our life, our sweetness, and our hope!
To you do we cry, poor banished children of Eve!
To you do we send up our sighs, mourning and weeping in this vale
of tears!
Turn then, most gracious advocate, your eyes of mercy toward us.
and after this, our exile, show unto us the blessed fruit of your womb,
Jesus!
O clement, O loving, O sweet Virgin Mary!
Pray for us, O Holy Mother of God,
that we may be made worthy of the promises of Christ. Amen.

Litany of the Blessed Virgin

Lord, have mercy on us.

Christ, have mercy on us.

Lord, have mercy on us.

Christ, hear us.

Christ, graciously hear us.

God, the Father of Heaven, have mercy on us.

God, the Son, Redeemer of the world, have mercy on us.

God, the Holy Spirit, have mercy on us.

Holy Trinity, one God, have mercy on us.

Holy Mary, pray for us.

Holy Mother of God, pray for us.

Holy Virgin of virgins, pray for us.

Mother of Christ, pray for us.

Mother of divine grace, pray for us.

Mother most pure, pray for us.

Mother most chaste, pray for us.

Mother inviolate, pray for us.

Mother undefiled, pray for us.

Mother most amiable, pray for us.

Mother most admirable, pray for us.

Mother of good counsel, pray for us.

Mother of our Creator, pray for us.

Mother of our Savior, pray for us.

Virgin most prudent, pray for us.

Virgin most venerable, pray for us.

Virgin most renowned, pray for us.

Virgin most powerful, pray for us.

Virgin most merciful, pray for us.

Virgin most faithful, pray for us.

Mirror of justice, pray for us.

Seat of wisdom, pray for us.

Cause of our joy, pray for us.

Spiritual vessel, pray for us.

Vessel of honor, pray for us.

Singular vessel of devotion, pray for us.

Mystical rose, pray for us.

Tower of David, pray for us.

Tower of ivory, pray for us.

House of gold, pray for us.

Ark of the covenant, pray for us.

Gate of heaven, pray for us.

Morning star, pray for us.

Health of the sick, pray for us.

Refuge of sinners, pray for us.

Comforter of the afflicted, pray for us.

Help of Christians, pray for us.

Queen of angels, pray for us.

Queen of patriarchs, pray for us.

Queen of prophets, pray for us.

Queen of apostles, pray for us.

Queen of martyrs, pray for us.

Queen of confessors, pray for us.

Queen of virgins, pray for us.

Queen of all saints, pray for us.

Queen conceived without original sin, pray for us.

Queen assumed into heaven, pray for us.

Queen of the most holy rosary, pray for us.

Queen of peace, pray for us.

Lamb of God, who takes away the sins of the world, Spare us, O Lord.

Lamb of God, who takes away the sins of the world,

Graciously hear us, O Lord.

Lamb of God, who takes away the sins of the world,

Have mercy on us.

Pray for us, O holy Mother of God,

That we may be made worthy of the promises of Christ.

Let us pray.

Grant, we beseech you, O Lord God, that we your servants may enjoy perpetual health of soul and body; and by the glorious intercession of blessed Mary, ever Virgin, may be delivered from present sorrows and rejoice in eternal happiness, through Christ, our Lord. Amen.

The Angelus

The angel of the Lord declared unto Mary:

And she conceived of the Holy Spirit.

Hail, Mary...

Behold the handmaid of the Lord:

Be it done unto me according to your word.

Hail, Mary...

And the Word was made flesh:

And dwelt among us.

Hail, Mary...

Pray for us, O holy Mother of God,

That we may be made worthy of the promises of Christ.

Let us pray.

Pour forth, we beseech you, O Lord, your grace into our hearts, that as we have known the incarnation of Christ your Son by the message of an angel, so by his passion and cross we may be brought to the glory of his resurrection, through the same Christ, our Lord. Amen.

Guardian Angel Prayer

Angel of God, my guardian dear,
To whom his love commits me here,
Ever this day be at my side,
To light and guard,
To rule and guide. Amen.

Patron Saints

Patrons of Occupations
Accountants: Matthew
Actors: Genesius
Artists: Catherine of Bologna, Fra Angelico
Aviators: John of Cupertino
Authors: Francis de Sales
Bakers: Elizabeth of Hungary
Bankers: Matthew
Booksellers: John of God
Businesswomen: Margaret Clitherow
Butchers: Antony of Egypt

Carpenters: Joseph
Catechists: Charles Borromeo
Construction: Stephen of Hungary
Cooks: Martha
Dentists: Apollonia
Doctors: Luke, Cosmas, and Damian
Editors: John Bosco
Farmers: Isidore
Florists: Thérèse of Lisieux
Fishermen: Andrew
Funeral directors: Joseph of Arimathea
Gardeners: Adelard
Grocers: Michael
Housewives: Anne
Jurists: John of Capistrano
Lawyers: Thomas More
Librarians: Jerome
Maids: Zita
Media: Archangel Gabriel
Musicians: Cecilia, Gregory the Great
Nurses: Agatha, Camillus de Lellis, Catherine of Siena
Pharmacists: Gemma Galgani
Priests: John Vianney
Public relations: Bernardine of Siena
Retreat masters: Ignatius of Loyola
Sailors: Brendan
Scientists: Albert the Great
Sculptors: Castorius
Social Workers: Louise de Marillac

Soldiers: George, Joan of Arc

Speakers: John Chrysostom

Stenographers: Cassian

Students: Thomas Aquinas

Teachers: Gregory the Great, John Baptiste de la Salle

Theologians: Alphonsus Liguori

Patrons in Special Circumstances

Adopted children: Clotilde

Alcoholism: Monica

Bachelors: Benedict Joseph Labre

Cancer: Peregrine

Child abuse victims: Alodia

Childlessness: Catherine of Siena

Converts: Helena

Death of children: Dorothy of Montau

Desperate situations: Rita

Difficult marriages: Fabiola, Catherine of Genoa, Elizabeth of Portugal

Expectant mothers: Gerard Majella

Eye disease: Lucy

Handicapped: Alphais

Headache: Teresa of Avila

Homelessness: Benedict Joseph Labre

Hunters: Hubert

Lost items: Anthony

Mental illness: Drogo, Dymphna

Migrants: Frances Xavier Cabrini

Motorists: Christopher

Orphans: Aurelius

Pilgrims: James

Rape victims: Agatha, Agnes, Maria Goretti

Second marriages: Adelaide

Sickness: Lydwine

Skiers: Bernard of Montjoux

Single laywomen: Agatha, Bibiana, Emiliana

Throat disease: Blaise

Widows: Angela of Foligno

Widowers: Edgar

Women in labor: Anne

Youth: Aloysius Gonzaga

Eleven

When the Night Is Over, Morning Comes

He put a new song in my mouth, a song of praise to our God.
Many will see and fear, and put their trust in the Lord.

PSALM 40:3

When a sudden crisis is finally, if not over, at least more bearable, we cry out, "Praise the Lord!" When through God's love we are victorious after a struggle that has lasted many years or even decades, we need to spend more than a few moments in thanksgiving. We know that there is no heaven on earth. We realize that more crosses are around the corner. But when one particular suffering is gone, we need to take a long pause to refresh ourselves.

What kind of refreshment do you need? Probably you need just to relax in the Lord and not do anything that isn't absolutely necessary. The more you know that even under the worst circumstances you have survived with the help of God, the more you can afford a little rest now and then.

Isn't it possible that Jesus himself wants you to be carefree and joyful for a while in the spirit of a Sabbath rest? Might he be disappointed if you just go from one crisis immediately on to worrying about future problems you anticipate? When Jesus said that our joy would be full (see Jn 15:11), don't you think he meant it?

Precisely because he has saved us from a great trouble, we should rejoice: "For great is his steadfast love toward us; and the faithfulness of the Lord endures for ever. Praise the Lord!" (Ps 117:2).

In the introduction, I wrote that God allows the sufferings you go through to draw you closer to himself, the only total Source of hope and joy. Part of your thanksgiving for a crisis passed needs to be a radical decision for holiness. After many crises past, here is my prayer for myself and for you:

"Dear Jesus, Mary, Joseph, and all the angels and saints, I thank you for all the ways you have seen me through crisis after crisis in my life. Some of those problems came from without, but many came from my own sins and imperfections. You know how likely I am to be overwhelmed again and feel unable to cope. At this moment I surrender my life to you. I am willing to bear any cross you choose to send to draw me closer to you. Please give me your strength when those times come.

"I pray that the Holy Spirit will supply special insight for the readers of this book, to make up for any omissions or errors of mine. Please direct them to further sources of wisdom, encouragement, and hope. And may we all someday meet in the place where you will dry all our tears and give us what no eye has seen or ear has heard: you yourself, in your glory!"

Books Cited

These books and those listed in the section called "Resources" can be found simply by calling any local bookstore. If they don't have a book you want, they can order it for you.

Catechism of the Catholic Church. 2nd ed. New York: Doubleday, 1997.

Dostoevsky, Fyodor. *The Brothers Karamazov,* trans. Constance Garnett. New York: Random House, 1977.

Dreikurs, Rudolf, and Pearl Cassel. *Discipline Without Tears.* New York: Mass Market, 1990.

Frankl, Viktor E. *Man's Search for Meaning.* New York: Mass Market, 1988.

John Paul II and Andre Frossard. *Be Not Afraid!* New York: St. Martin's, 1984.

Lewis, C.S. *The Problem of Pain.* New York: Collier/Simon and Schuster, 1978.

von Hildebrand, Dietrich. *Jaws of Death: Gate of Heaven.* Manchester, N.H.: Sophia Institute, 1991.

———. *Transformation in Christ: On the Christian Attitude.* Manchester, N.H.: Sophia Institute, 2001.

Wojtyla, Karol (John Paul II). *Love and Responsibility.* San Francisco: Ignatius, 1996.

Resources

This is a list of books and other resources I recommend and that you might find helpful. It is not meant to be complete in any way.

General

Catechism of the Catholic Church. 2nd ed. New York: Doubleday, 1997.

Chervin, Ronda, ed. *Holding Hands With God.* Oak Lawn, Ill.: CMJ Marian, 2000. Stories by women about surviving terrible crosses.

———. *Living in Love: About Christian Ethics.* Boston: Pauline, 1989. Includes chapters on the most controversial issues such as contraception.

———. *Signs of Love: About the Sacraments.* Boston: Pauline, 1988.

Chervin, Ronda, and Gary Hagins. *How to Be a Total Catholic.* Oak Lawn, Ill.: CMJ Marian, 2001.

John Paul II and Andre Frossard. *Be Not Afraid!* New York: St. Martin's, 1984.

Porter, Ross, and Ronda Chervin. *Meditations on the Gospel of St. John.* Oak Lawn, Ill.: CMJ Marian, 2001.

Schreck, Alan. *Catholic and Christian: An Explanation of Commonly Misunderstood Catholic Beliefs.* Ann Arbor, Mich.: Servant, 1984.

von Hildebrand, Dietrich. *Transformation in Christ: On the Christian Attitude.* Manchester, N.H.: Sophia Institute Press, 2001.

About Specific Needs and Topics

Addictions and Compulsions

Consult the phone books for various twelve-step programs in your area such as Alcoholics Anonymous, Overeaters Anonymous, Co-da (for co-dependency), and so on. Usually anyone you call will know the numbers for other programs such as Gambler's or Nicotine Anonymous.

Harvey, John F. *The Homosexual Person: New Thinking in Pastoral Care.* San Francisco: Ignatius, 1987.

May, Gerald. *Addiction and Grace: Love and Spirituality in the Healing of Addiction.* San Francisco: Harper, 1991.

O'Neill, Cherry Boone, and Dan O'Neill, with Paul Thigpen. *Living on the Border of Disorder: How to Cope With an Addictive Person.* Minneapolis: Bethany, 1992.

Aging

Chervin, Ronda. *Seeking Christ in the Crosses and Joys of Aging.* Oak Lawn, Ill.: CMJ Marian, 2001.

Angels

Parente, Pascal P. *The Angels: The Catholic Teaching on the Angels.* Rockford, Ill.: TAN, 1973.

Anger

The best method I have ever found for dealing with anger is to go to one of the by-donation-only groups that meet all over the world called Recovery, Inc. Even though it is not religious, it is sound from a natural point of view. You can find a group near you by calling Recovery, Inc., in Chicago at 312-337-5661.

Death of Loved Ones

Chervin, Ronda, ed. *Holding Hands With God.* Oak Lawn, Ill.: CMJ Marian, 2000.

Chervin, Ronda. *En Route to Eternity.* Ann Arbor, Mich.: Miriam Press, 1995. This autobiography includes a chapter about my son's suicide.

Lewis, C.S. *A Grief Observed.* San Francisco: Harper, 1994.

Eucharistic Adoration

Hardon, Fr. John, S.J. *The History of Eucharistic Adoration.* Oak Lawn, Ill.: CMJ Marian, 1997. A long booklet, extremely informative and useful in convincing doubters.

Thigpen, Paul, comp. *Jesus, We Adore You: Prayers Before the Blessed Sacrament.* Ann Arbor, Mich.: Servant, 2001. A collection of prayers and meditations for Eucharistic adoration.

Fear of Death

Chervin, Ronda. *Victory Over Death.* Oak Lawn, Ill.: CMJ Marian, 2001.

von Hildebrand, Dietrich. *Jaws of Death: Gate of Heaven.* Manchester, N.H.: Sophia Institute, 1991.

Forgiveness

Thigpen, Paul. *The Saints' Guide to Making Peace With God, Yourself, and Others.* Ann Arbor, Mich.: Servant, 2001. Wisdom from the saints for healing your relationships.

God's Existence

Chervin, Ronda. "A Contemporary Look at Old Arguments for God's Existence." New Hope, Ky.: Faith Guild, n.d. To order, call 800-789-9494. This leaflet contains proofs for God's existence from prominent scientists.

Chervin, Ronda, and Lois Janis. *Voyage to Insight.* Oak Lawn, Ill.: CMJ Marian, 2000. This book about discovering your own philosophy of life contains refutations of general skepticism and also proofs for God's existence.

Mary

Chervin, Ronda. *Mary: Teach Us How to Live.* Oak Lawn, Ill.: CMJ Marian, 2001.

Hahn, Scott. *Hail, Holy Queen: The Mother of God in the Word of God.* New York: Doubleday, 2001.

von Speyr, Adrienne. *Handmaid of the Lord.* San Francisco: Ignatius, 1985.

Natural Family Planning

Kippley, John F. and Sheila K. Kippley. *The Art of Natural Family Planning.* Cincinnati, Ohio: Couple to Couple League, 1989. The best book on why contraception is wrong and why NFP works and is better. Call them also for information about the nearest league couple for classes.

Prayer

For an easy way to get closer to God in prayer, try ordering the magazine *Magnificat.* It offers wonderful meditations on the daily liturgical scriptural texts. Write: *Magnificat,* P.O. Box 91, Spencerville, MD 20868.

An excellent way to enter into a more contemplative prayer life is to read the great masters such as St. Teresa of Avila, St. John of the Cross, and St. Francis de Sales. Books by them can be found in your parish library or any Catholic bookstore.

Chervin, Ronda. *Hungry for Heaven: The Biography of Charles Rich, Lay Contemplative.* Petersham, Mass.: St. Bede's, 1987. The story of a Jewish convert who influenced many people to pray more deeply.

Chervin, Ronda. *Prayers of the Women Mystics.* Ann Arbor, Mich.: Servant, 1992.

Dubay, Thomas. *Fire Within.* San Francisco: Ignatius, 1989. Shows how the prayer of the great mystics is an exemplification of the Gospel.

Lewis, C. S. *Letters to Malcolm: Chiefly on Prayer.* New York: Harcourt, Brace, Jovanovich, 1963.

Thigpen, Paul, comp. *The Prayers of Pope John Paul II.* Ann Arbor, Mich.: Servant, 1996.

The Saints

Butler's Lives of the Saints. Rev. ed. by Herbert J. Thurston, J.S. and Donald Attwater. Westminster, Md.: Christian Classics, 1988.

Chervin, Ronda. *Quotable Saints.* Oak Lawn, Ill.: CMJ Marian, 2000.

Chervin, Ronda. *Treasury of Women Saints.* Ann Arbor, Mich.: Servant, 1991.

Cruz, Joan Carroll. *Secular Saints.* Rockford, Ill.: TAN, 1989.

Freze, Michael. *Patron Saints.* Huntington, Ind.: Our Sunday Visitor, 1995.

Hess, Heidi S., comp. *Let Nothing Trouble You: 60 Reflections From the Writings of St. Teresa of Avila.* Ann Arbor, Mich.: Servant, 1998.

Thigpen, Paul, comp. *Be Merry in God: 60 Reflections From the Writings of St. Thomas More.* Ann Arbor, Mich.: Servant, 1999.

———, comp. *A Dictionary of Quotes From the Saints.* Ann Arbor, Mich.: Servant, 2001.

———, comp. *Restless Till We Rest in You: 60 Reflections From the Writings of St. Augustine.* Ann Arbor, Mich.: Servant, 1998.

van Balen Holt, Mary, comp. *A Dwelling Place Within: 60 Reflections From the Writings of St. Francis of Assisi.* Ann Arbor, Mich.: Servant, 1999.

Suffering

Chervin, Ronda. *Kiss from the Cross: A Saint for Every Kind of Suffering.* Ann Arbor, Mich.: Servant, 1994.

Kreeft, Peter. *Making Sense Out of Suffering.* Ann Arbor, Mich.: Servant, 1986.

Lewis, C.S. *The Problem of Pain.* New York: Collier/Simon and Schuster, 1978.

Thigpen, Paul. *Blood of the Martyrs, Seed of the Church: Stories of Catholics Who Died for Their Faith.* Ann Arbor, Mich.: Servant, 2001.

Widowhood

Chervin, Ronda. *A Widow's Walk: Encouragement, Wisdom, and Comfort from the Widow Saints.* Huntington, Ind.: Our Sunday Visitor, 1998.

Index